TAPESTRY OF YESTERYEAR

TAPESTRY OF YESTERYEAR

Growing up on Pilley's Island

Gwendolyn Poole Molnar

FLANKER PRESS LTD.
ST. JOHN'S
2009

Library and Archives Canada Cataloguing in Publication

Poole Molnar, Gwendolyn, 1915-
Tapestry of yesteryear : growing up on Pilley's Island / Gwendolyn Poole Molnar.

ISBN 978-1-897317-49-5

1. Poole Molnar, Gwendolyn, 1915- --Childhood and youth. 2. Pilley's Island (N.L.)--Social life and customs--20th century. 3. Pilley's Island (N.L.)--Biography. I. Title.

FC2199.P525Z49 2009 971.8'02092 C2009-903847-1

PRINTED IN CANADA

FLANKER PRESS
P.O. BOX 2522, STATION C
ST. JOHN'S, NL A1C 6K1 CANADA
TOLL-FREE: 1-866-739-4420
WWW.FLANKERPRESS.COM

Cover Design: Adam Freake
Cover image: Left to right, Madge, Gwen and Geneva (Neve)

14 13 12 11 10 09 1 2 3 4 5 6 7 8 9

Canada

Canada Council for the Arts | Conseil des Arts du Canada

Newfoundland Labrador

We acknowledge the financial support of: the Government of Canada through the Book Publishing Industry Development Program (BPIDP); the Canada Council for the Arts which last year invested $20.1 million in writing and publishing throughout Canada; the Government of Newfoundland and Labrador, Department of Tourism, Culture and Recreation.

Encouraged by my brother Don, niece Janice (Wells), and cousin Cyril, I feel a deep urgency to record the events of my childhood, in Pilley's Island, Notre Dame Bay, Newfoundland, as I remember them, before the shadows close in on me and I can no longer visualize them as I see them so clearly today.

I dedicate this chronicle to my children, Gail and Paul, my granddaughter Christy, my great-grandson Carlton Carter III, my great-granddaughter Rileigh Gwendolyn Dunn, and the children and grandchildren of my sister Gladys, my sister Geneva (Wells), my sister Madge (Steeves), and my brother Don, and also to my cousins Roy, Una (Payne), Cyril, Winston, Joyce (Danhof), Mervyn, and Ed and their children and grandchildren, and to the descendants of my aunts Bertha, Lena, Ethel, and Lillian.

Gwen Molnar
North Tonawanda, N.Y.
1993

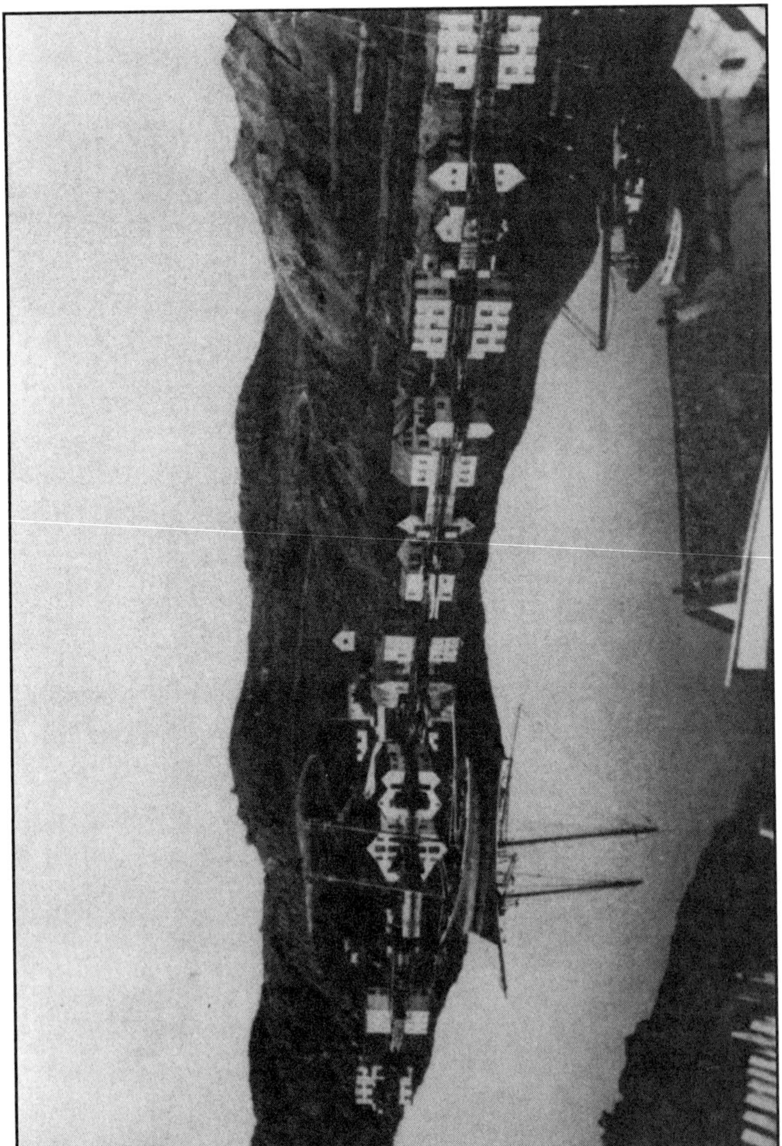

Contents

To Pop

And now at last the tired old warrior rests,
His fight is ended, his last course is run;
His like we'll see no more, he was the best,
The world seems very empty since he's gone.

We would not, if we could, disturb his sleep,
We're only happy that his suffering's o'er;
We should not, must not mourn! And yet we weep,
For a way of life that was and is no more.

His childlike saintliness has surely earned
Triumphant rise while death's shadows fall,
And now, safe home, he truly will have learned,
To know at last "The Wonder of It All."

He fathered five, yet twelve were in his heart,
He showed all twelve affection, love and trust;
And with his going, took with him a part,
A great big part of every one of us.

Goodbye dear Pop! Goodbye dear Uncle Jess!
We'll keep remembering till memories cease;
We give your soul to God, He'll do the rest,
We loved you well Old-Timer! Rest in Peace!

Home is the hunter, home from the hill,
And the sailor home from the sea.

Gwen Poole Molnar
1977

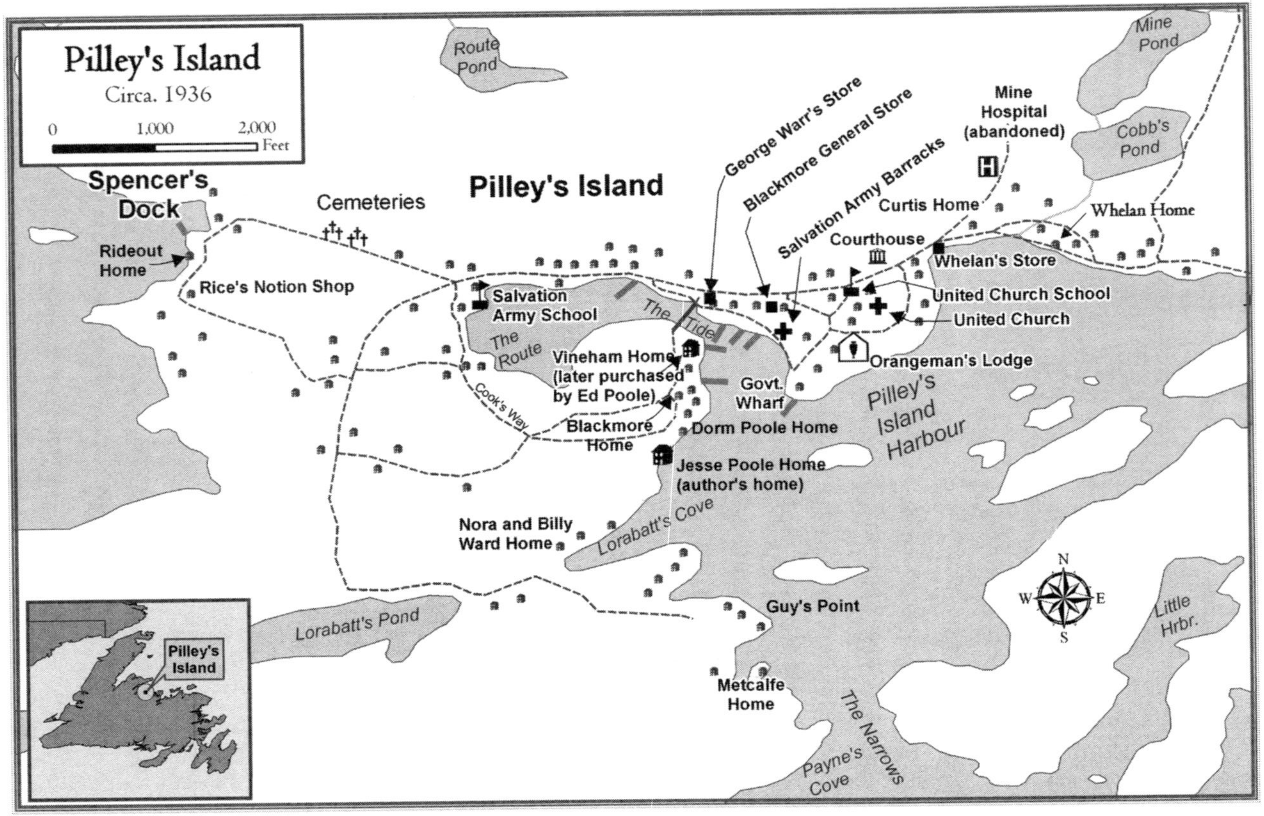
Pilley's Island
Circa. 1936
0
1,000
2,000
Feet
Route Pond
Mine Pond
Cobb's Pond
Spencer's Dock
Rideout Home
Cemeteries
Pilley's Island
Rice's Notion Shop
George Warr's Store
Blackmore General Store
Salvation Army Barracks
Mine Hospital (abandoned)
Curtis Home
Whelan Home
Courthouse
Whelan's Store
United Church School
United Church
Orangeman's Lodge
Salvation Army School
The Route
The Tide
Vineham Home (later purchased by Ed Poole)
Cook's Way
Govt. Wharf
Blackmore Home
Dorm Poole Home
Jesse Poole Home (author's home)
Pilley's Island Harbour
Lorabatt's Cove
Nora and Billy Ward Home
Lorabatt's Pond
Guy's Point
N
W
E
S
Little Hrbr.
Pilley's Island
Metcalfe Home
The Narrows
Payne's Cove

Foreword

My aunt Gwen, to whom I dedicated my first book, *The Gin & Tonic Gardener,* is now in her ninety-fifth year and can still beat me at Scrabble. Last year, for the first time in years, I reread her *Tapestry of Yesteryear*, which was written originally only for her family. I was struck by the difference between this work and many others about that era in outport Newfoundland, which, while no doubt accurate, focus more on the hardship and coarseness of the time and do not capture the peacefulness and charm that were also very real, particularly through the eyes of a child.

Purely coincidental to her title, I believe my aunt's memoir adds a valuable little thread to the tapestry of Newfoundland social history. I was so pleased when Garry and Margo Cranford at Flanker Press agreed with me and I am happy and honoured to have played a role in the publishing of the first book of an unsung daughter of Newfoundland.

Janice Wells
St. John's, 2009

My heartfelt thanks go to my niece Janice Wells for her confidence and editing, my nephew David Poole for the fine map of Pilley's Island and to all the family members who contributed memory and photographs to the final version, to my daughter Gail Andress, granddaughter Christy Dunn and niece Karin Brown for transcribing. Thank you also to the Green Bay Development Association and others in the Pilley's Island area who tried to help, to Peter Hanes at Flanker Press for his work in reproducing the old photographs, and to Flanker Press for seeing value in these memories.

Life Was Tenuous

It is a miracle that I survived my birth and am alive to tell this tale. My mother went into labour on a sultry August morning in 1915 attended by the local midwife, Aunt Lizzie Simms, and a couple of well-meaning neighbours. (Later with my knowledge as a maternity nurse, I presumed I must have been a breach birth.) In any event, when I finally emerged, blue and still, the good souls just dropped me on the bed in the next room and gave all their attention to my weak, exhausted mother.

Just about that time, another neighbour, Aunt Jane Cook arrived. Most older people were called aunts or uncles though in reality were not related at all. She saw the frenzied activity as the women worked on my mother. Then it dawned on her that something was missing. "Where is the baby?" she asked. "Oh, the baby is dead. She's in the other room." Aunt Jane decided to see for herself and that is when she saw the faintest flutter of my eyelids. With great dispatch she produced two pans of water, one hot and one cold, and proceeded to dunk me from one into the other, until I emitted a feeble squawk. From then on it was all uphill. My mother revived and was happy to hear that little Gwendolyn Dorothy was alive and kicking, thanks to the ministrations of Aunt Jane Cook, who from that day on held a special place in my mother's heart.

All went well and my two older sisters, Gladys, five, and Geneva, nearly four, were delighted with their baby sister. In fact, Gladys was so delighted that when I was a week old and my mother's back was turned, she gathered me up in her arms. She was presumably taking me for my first airing when – whoops! – she dropped me on the doorstep. When my mother came weakly tottering up, Gladys looked up with an angelic smile and said, "It's all right, Mommy, it was only her head that struck." There were no doctors, no X-rays, and presumably no cranial damage. Hearing that story in later years, I blamed all my faults and failures on that one crack on the head.

I was a placid baby and thrived on breast-feeding, my only blemish being my left eye, which was slightly crossed. To quote my mother, "It had a cast in it." It was very noticeable in early childhood. In fact, my very first memory is when I was a chubby three-year-old playing with Ada Rideout, who lived nearby. From her advanced age of five, she looked down her nose at me and said, "You'd be pretty if you didn't have a crossed eye." I was shattered. Quite likely, that remark was responsible for the inferiority complex that dogged the years of my youth.

My mother, Mildred Alcock, was born in Leading Tickles, two hours away by motorboat, the child of Mary Jane Budgell and Robert Dudley Alcock. I know little about them, except that Grandfather Alcock was a well-read aristocratic-looking gentleman whom my mother always addressed as "sir."[1] At some point Mary Jane died and her father remarried. My mother called this woman "madam" and, when she too died, forever after referred to her as "poor madam."

When she was eighteen, my mother came to Pilley's Island to live with her uncle, Will Budgell and soon after that she met my father. He proposed to her in Uncle Will's front parlour and soon they were married.

My father was born in 1883 in Sop's Arm, the first son of Edward Poole of Hant's Harbour and

1 - Based on research done in later years by Gladys, family lore has Robert Dudley Alcock being a descendant of Robert Dudley, first Earl of Leicester and favourite of Queen Elizabeth I. Elizabeth refused to marry Dudley but became outraged when he had liaisons with other women in the court. On one occasion when a lady-in-waiting became pregnant, Elizabeth shipped her off to the New World, where she landed in Harbour Grace, Newfoundland, she gave birth to a son she named Robert Dudley, the first of a long line of Newfoundland males to bear that name. The family once owned a picture of the Queen Mother with her attendants on a balcony at Buckingham Palace, one of whom was the image of Geneva.

Lucy Way of Herring Neck. He never had any formal education. As a child, education took second place to working with his father. When he was about six, his father would take him to help with the nets. If he were caught dozing on his oars, Grandpa would flick salt water in his face. Hearing that story, my heart ached for the little boy that he was. Somehow, I couldn't make the connection between that and the kindly, gentle grandfather that I knew and loved. But times were harsh in the days of my father's boyhood and children were treated accordingly.

In the early months of their marriage, my mother, with great optimism, set out to teach him to read and write; she would get pencil, slate, and books on the table, but halfway through the lesson, my father would be snoring in his chair. Time after time this was repeated, until finally, frustrated and in tears, my mother abandoned the project, and so my father, a man with a natural intelligence that impressed all who knew him, lived out his ninety-five years able only to sign his name

When I was very little, we shared a house with Grandpa and Grandma Poole, and Aunts Lillian and Ethel. They lived in the one side, we lived in the other. There was no connection between the two sides, and we had to go outside around the back to Grandma's. We each had a large kitchen and "front room" downstairs, two bedrooms and a large hall and stairway upstairs. The house was built under a hill. It had three-quarters of the foundation on the ground, the other quarter over the water on a breastwork of large logs. It was in a land-locked harbour, and when wind arose, we would lie awake and hear the waves crashing against the house. When I was old enough, I slept between Gladys and Geneva. During a storm we would lie in bed and cuddle up, so deliciously safe and snug, while we felt sorry for anyone out in that wild Atlantic night.

Grandma was a pretty woman, with high cheekbones and raven hair. She was very intelligent, and when she was sixteen her parents decided to send her to England to finish her education. But then she met and married Edward Poole, and that was that. I'm sure she never regretted it as they were supremely happy. The next year my father, Jesse, was born and the others followed in quick succession, twelve children in all.

Before I went to school, I spent a lot of time with Grandma. She was a fountain of Bible knowledge. I adored her and loved nestling in her lap while she told me Bible stories. I was devastated when she died of cancer at the age of fifty-two. With no merciful drugs to alleviate her pain, she lay patiently in bed, never complaining, and always welcoming us with a smile. She had religious mottos all over her bedroom walls. One day, when my sister Geneva stole a grape from her bedside stand, her eyes fell on a motto which said, "Be sure your sins will find you out." I have no idea where the grapes came from; they were like gold dust to us, and I wouldn't touch them for anything. According to Geneva, that grape was bitter gall in her mouth.

After weeks of growing steadily weaker and thinner, Grandma died as quietly and unobtrusively as she lived. Grandpa himself made her coffin. I stood and watched as he worked with skilful, loving hands, and with tears streaming down his cheeks. I was ten years old.

I loved my grandfather as much as my grandmother but in a different way I think I was Grandpa's favourite, perhaps because I had inherited his eye defect, or perhaps because I took his lunch to him every day as he made barrels at Blackmore's Cooper Shop. I wore a yellow pinafore a lot and he used to call me his little yellowhammer. I didn't mind the tickling of his bristly moustache when he kissed me.

When I was four, he made me a doll's cradle for Christmas. I can see that cradle still, and it was a beauty! It had rockers and was stained with rosewood varnish. It was my most prized possession. I was just as happy as if the doll I placed in it had been new, and not my sister's hand-me-down, but we were easily pleased.

After Grandma died, my father changed the house a bit, making connecting doors, so that now we had four rooms downstairs and four upstairs. Aunt Ethel had already left home to go teaching, and Aunt Lillian and Grandpa lived with us. My mother was pregnant with my brother Don, who was born in March, and Grandpa died in April. He, too, had the dreaded disease, but he faded so quickly after Grandma's death that everyone said he died of a broken heart. Their devotion to each other had been a beautiful thing. When he was laid out in his purple shroud, I kissed his cold cheek and whispered, "Goodbye, Grandpa, I love you."

Our Own Little World

Pilley's Island! How can I describe it? Even after a lapse of seventy years, I can see it all through the eyes of a seven-year-old. You could walk from one end to the other, from Spencer's Dock to Bumble Bee Bight, in about an hour. The homes were scattered along the waterfront, a few more inland in an area we called "the route."

We lived on Poole's Point. We were the last house on the road across "the bar," so-called because the tide ran under it, beginning up in the "route" and flowing out to the harbour. Directly over the tide was a bridge with railings. We would linger there, leaning over to watch the ceaseless flow of the water.

By this time we were Gladys, Geneva, Gwen, Madge, and Don. The next-to-last house and just a stone's throw away from ours belonged to Uncle Dorm and Aunt Blanche.

My father and Uncle Dorm were brothers and partners. Dorm was four years younger (another brother in between died in infancy) and they did everything together. They owned a sawmill, had a small canning factory, trapped and hunted in the fall and winter, fished and logged in the summer. Uncle Dorm had a brief marriage to Maggie Pittman, their offspring being Roy and Una. I faintly remember Aunt Maggie, who died of tuberculosis. She was quiet and introverted, the direct opposite of his second wife, Blanche Watkins, who was bubbly and outgoing and whom we all adored. In due time were born Cyril, Winston, Joyce, Mervyn, and Edward.

The two families were so closely knit that I've always considered my cousins an extended part of my own family, especially Joyce, some fourteen years younger than I, who seemed like an adored little sister.

Pilley's Island had a population of around six hundred people in 1920, when I was five. A lot of people died in the flu epidemic after World War I, but our family escaped. Everyone knew everyone else, with older people being called aunts and uncles, as in Uncle Eleazer and Aunt Leah Weir, Uncle Phil and Aunt Susie Vineham, Uncle Tom and Aunt Cis Rowsell, and all the others.

We were poor, but then, so was everyone else and we didn't feel greatly deprived. Money was scarce, but there wasn't the demand for money that there is today. Everyone owned his own home so there was no mortgage or homeowner's insurance, no electric, gas, water, telephone, or TV cable bills. There were no city, town, or school taxes, and for the most part, people gained their subsistence off the land, the lumber woods, and the fisheries.

Our only source of communication with the outside world was by coastal steamer in summer and dog team in winter. A big thrill was looking forward to seeing the weekly steamer arrive. I remember a succession of steamers. First the SS *Home*, then the SS *Clyde*, and later the SS *Springdale*, made weekly trips from Lewisporte, calling in Exploits, Fortune Harbour, Cottles Cove, Leading Tickles, Triton, and Brighton, finally arriving at Pilley's Island, then on to points north, calling back in three days en route to Lewisporte again.

These steamer arrivals had a big effect on my life. As I stood on the government wharf while the ships glided in and I caught glimpses of people at the ship's rail, I had my first introduction to what another life could possibly be, away from our tight little island. When the ships appeared in the narrows at night, with lights gleaming, chains clanking, and the hustle and bustle of the crew, I longed to be a passenger. Our house was near the government wharf, and, as the ship backed out to depart, I could see the people standing on the stern deck. They seemed so near I could almost touch them. In later years as I would go home on vacations from nursing school, I would stand on that same stern deck and see my mother standing on the verandah and waving like mad.

In addition to the excitement of the ship's arrival was the tense air of expectancy as we proceeded to the office to get our mail. This might have been a letter or two from relatives in other parts of Newfoundland, or Eaton's catalogue from Toronto, which we all peered over for nights and nights. The biggest attraction of all was the *Family Herald and Weekly Star*, a newspaper to which my mother subscribed faithfully and which held a world of information. My mother's favourite was Dorothy Dix, the equivalent of today's Ann Landers. Geneva and I were addicts of the Maple Leaf Club Pen Pal page.

Geneva wrote for pen pals, signing herself "Circe." Her letter flowed and was so eloquent that she received a deluge of letters, but couldn't answer them all as the postage was three cents and way out of our league. She did keep up correspondence with a certain Kenneth Albright from New Brunswick. As time went on he became quite amorous, and Geneva spent long hours writing her heart out in pages and pages of eloquence to Kenneth. Eventually, as such things will, the romance petered out.

My pen name was Laughing Water, and I kept up a small flow of correspondence with a few of the many who responded, the longest being with a W. Lionel Smith from Toronto, who sent me his picture. He was rather handsome except for a beaklike nose, but I overlooked that and kept letters going back and forth, until I left the island for greener pastures.

Another section of the *Family Herald and Weekly Star*, which we all loved and fought to read first, was the weekly serial, "The White Cottage Mystery." My mother usually got at it first, then on to us and we would discuss it at length, imagining what the next episode would be. I think my joy of reading originated with the *Family Herald and Weekly Star*.

After the harbour froze solid and ships could no longer get in through the narrows, the mail arrived weekly by dog team. There was great suspense wondering just when the dogsled would arrive. When at last it came into view and it passed our house, we could count the bags of mail and wondered what small percentage, if any, would be for us. Just one thing was a constant, our beloved *Family Herald and Weekly Star*. We did the puzzles, entered the contests, and eagerly read up on the little princesses, Elizabeth and Margaret. There wasn't a line that wasn't avidly perused.

Our only means of getting daily news was by going to the post office and reading the report that our postmistress, Ivy Curtis, obtained through wireless telegraphy. It was a three-page report written in her inimitable style in a ledger that was always available to the public. It told, in brief, news from around the world, the weather report, and local temperatures. There was no radio or crystal set in any home on Pilley's Island until the early 1930s.

Boats – not cars or bicycles – were our common and regular way of travel. Three steps descended into the water from our verandah, and our rowboat was tied up there. We used it all the time for errands, for berry picking or just for leisurely rows up and down the harbour or sometimes farther afield. Our front verandah was built over the water, so that, when the tide was high, we could fish for tomcods from there.

My father didn't often take time out for pleasure trips, but I remember one weekend when I was around four, they decided to visit Leading Tickles where my mother's family, and her father, Grandpa Alcock, still lived. Aunt Nora Ward, who also had relatives there, decided to go along with us. I think it may have been a three-hour drive. We arrived safely and I had a great time playing with Cousin Annie and walking out to the lighthouse, where Cousin Arch Martin was the keeper.

We went in the big open skiff. Pop had rigged up a tarpaulin to make a shelter for my mother, Aunt Nora, and me. We were about halfway home when the motor conked out, as they did so often in those days. My father had little mechanical ability. Uncle Dorm was always the engineer, but now Pop was alone and had to rely on his own efforts.

My mother and Aunt Nora, both deathly seasick, were lying on blankets in the bottom of the boat whilst I kept nervous vigil. Pop was tinkering in the engine room, and we drifted helplessly, when suddenly, the boat crashed into a cliff. The boat sustained no damage, but my father's head hit the engine with a bang. When my mother heard the crash and looked up to see blood streaming down my father's face, she jumped up, her seasickness forgotten, tore up her petticoat to bandage Pop's head, then grasped the tiller while Aunt Nora just lay there in a semi-comatose state.

Pop threw out the anchor to slow the drifting – how long it lasted, we couldn't tell. It seemed forever, until we were spied by a fishing boat and towed back home to Pilley's. Mom and I clambered on the wharf's railing, happy to be home. Aunt Nora had to be helped up by my father and Uncle Dorm, who had come out to meet us. She then collapsed on the wharf, a sorry bundle! After getting her second wind, she tottered in to our house and lay on the kitchen couch until her husband, Uncle Billy, arrived to take her home.

My mother vowed never to visit Leading Tickles via motorboat again. And ever after, she made her annual summer pilgrimage on the SS *Home*. The ship really belied its name, being anything but like home. We always went steerage, which we shared with other hapless passengers and a scattered bedbug here and there. Mom always carried her old black hat tin, a startling contrast to the sleek luggage of today.

Aunt Blanche, whose family lived in Head's Harbour, would sometimes ask me to accompany her on her visits home, as her rowing partner. We would pick a sunny day, with just a light breeze rippling the water, and with her manning the fore paddles and me confidently grasping the aft paddles, we would set out. As we rowed down the tickle that runs between Pilley's Island and Head's Harbour, I never tired of gazing at the sheer beauty of the deeply forested hills reflected in the water. A royal procession of birch, spruce, and aspen stood like silent sentinels as we passed.

When we reached Head's Harbour and tied up at the wharf leading up to the Watkins home, we were greeted by a noisy tribe of children, Watkinses and Fudges, all nephews and nieces of Aunt Blanche. Her mother was a sweet, refined lady who always made me welcome.

Pilley's Island now has a causeway connecting it to the mainland, and another connecting it with Head's Harbour (Triton Island), passable roads for cars, and such modern conveniences as electricity and indoor plumbing. In all my growing-up years from 1915 to 1936, when, after working in Warr's and Blackmore's stores for a few years, I left to enter Grace Hospital Training School for Nurses in St. John's, it was a simple, primitive, uncomplicated existence, and happy for the most part.

There Were No Strangers

Beginning in Spencer's Dock, I shall try to describe most of the residents, some of their virtues and vices, and also the whimsies with which each family was plentifully endowed.

There were two parts to Spencer's Dock. In one lived the Rices and the Denneys, two families of each and all cousins of ours. Grandmother Poole, Aunt Mary Jane Rice, and Aunt Lizzie Denney were sisters. We had a legal right to the term of "Auntie" in this instance. Uncle John Denney (Aunt Lizzie's husband) had huge whiskers that bristled merrily as he beat on the "big drum" in the Salvation Army barracks on Sunday morning and again in the evening.

Like my grandmother, Aunt Lizzie was a teller of tales. We were held spellbound as she told stories of her youth, and shivered deliciously as she expanded on ghosts, spirits, lights, and tokens. We would be delighted when we heard Aunt Lizzie was coming to stay overnight. She would mend and darn and knit, her eyes twinkling as she held us all in thrall. Aunt Lizzie and Uncle John had two sons, Albert and Elias, great buddies of my father, being about the same age. They each had a houseful of children. Sadie and Ethel were closest to my age, and Minnie and Geneva were great friends. The Rices also had two sons, Sidney and Arthur, plus several daughters, who in turn married and had children that were our peers and went to school with us.

Albert Denney was a favourite of mine because he was so funny and witty. On Sunday mornings after service, Pop would often invite Albert to dinner, and even my mother would relax and enjoy Albert and his funny stories.

Another family of Rices lived in the first part of Spencer's Dock, Uncle John and Aunt Fanny (no relation, however). Aunt Fanny had a small notions shop, and my mother would walk all the way to Spencer's Dock to save one cent on a roll of sewing cotton. They had one adopted daughter, Violet, who was Geneva's age, and Geneva, Violet, and Minnie Denney became a familiar threesome.

A little farther up the "bottom" lived a family of Ryans. I don't remember much about them except that they had a daughter with the improbable name of Idella.

A rocky road along the shore led one to the second part of Spencer's Dock. Here lived the Rideouts, Uncle Alfred and Aunt Lydia and their brood. Uncle Alfred had a good job as a pulpwood contractor for the A.N.D. Company, so they were a few notches above us in wealth. Winnie and I were in the same grades at school. She was a very pretty girl and I was most envious, because not only had she looks, but the money to buy an apple or candy at recess time. She was generous in wanting to share but I always declined; my pride wouldn't let me accept. The older daughter, Effie, was in training as a nurse at the General Hospital in St. John's, and one day I accepted Winnie's invitation to lunch at her home. Effie showed me her nurse's pin, and then and there I made up my mind I'd have one like it someday. There were also three sons, Pearce, Roland, Harold, and later, a baby sister, Marion. Just up the road were the Snows and the Lockes. Aunt Lil Locke was a sister to Alfred Rideout.

Farther on, in a little house built closer to the water and surrounded by trees and a front garden filled with red and black currants, lived Uncle Tom and Aunt Cis Rowsell. They had a daughter Bride, short for Bridget, and sons Pearce, Ford, Walter, and Vonnie. Uncle Tom was a gruff, dominant man, but good-hearted. Aunt Cis was a meek, sweet woman who seemed to be completely in her husband's shadow.

Geneva and I were always welcome to help ourselves to currants, and many a long, lazy summer afternoon was spent in Aunt Cis's front garden to the music of the Atlantic breakers, and the humming of the bees in the orchard. We would arrive home, sunburned and happy, and soon the kitchen would be redolent of the delicious aroma of currants cooking on the stove. Then Mom would carefully bottle and mark them for next winter's consumption.

The house that I remember most vividly in Spencer's Dock belonged to Aunt Kizzie and Uncle Mattie Callahan. They were both most eccentric and excellent book material. They owned a lot of land and their hills were filled with blueberry bushes which we were allowed to pick. My mother usually went with us as she loved to pick blueberries.

Aunt Kizzie would wrap groceries, put her name on them, and put them under the communal Christmas tree in the Orange Lodge where, after the Christmas concert was over, Santa would arrive and dispense the gifts. Aunt Kizzie's name was always called out, thanks to her own ingenuity.

Uncle Mattie in his latter days had a vision that there was gold buried near his house. He began digging a hole that seemed to stretch from here to eternity. People came from all over to see the wonder of Uncle Mattie's hole. As time went on, the interest waned as did Uncle Mattie's lust for life. He died a frustrated old man.

They had two children: a son, Cecil, and a daughter, Lizzie, who was married to Hedley Forsey. Not long after her death, Hedley was heard confiding to a crony, "First 'twas sorrow, then 'twas nature," as his desire to get on with life apparently took over.

Retracing our steps, we see the one-room schoolhouse on our right, the marsh where beautiful blue and white violets abounded, and the running brook where we filled our small water bottles for cleaning our slates. Through reconstruction and rebuilding, the once colourful marsh and the running brook have long since vanished, but I can see, smell, and hear them still. From the schoolhouse was a shortcut over the hills to our house, called "Cook's way." A couple of houses dotted the grassy path, one being that of Aunt Jane Cook previously mentioned.

Backtracking and coming down the "route," we pass the home of Aunt Polly and Uncle Billy Ryan. Their son Nathan later married Ella Verge, a childhood friend of Gladys. Nathan was quite intelligent, and his testimonies in prayer meeting waxed long and eloquent. Aunt Polly was somewhat of a harridan, constantly finding fault with the schoolchildren and their antics. When we were playing ball near the school, one of the boys, often cousin Roy, would bat the ball over her fence and Aunt Polly would get in one of her royal rages. The culprit would quickly retrieve the ball, and we'd take to our heels and not hear too much of her diatribe.

On the right and under the hill lived the Huskins family, and next door Uncle Eleazer and Aunt Leah Weir. She was a friendly, garrulous soul, and we loved to visit her at recess time. She would fill our stomachs with molasses bread and her own good cow's milk, and our ears with stories of Sop's Arm, where they had been neighbours of my grandparents, long ago, before they moved to Pilley's Island. Aunt Leah's tales were always well-embellished, and it was very hard to distinguish fact from fiction. Later we would obtain the true story from my father.

Then came the Harrises, Aaron and Selena. Aunt Selena's garden was a riot of colour: hollyhocks, tiger lilies, sweet william, roses, geraniums, fuchsias, phlox, pansies, sweet peas, and boy's love. I would lean over the fence on my way home from school and gaze in longing at the flowers. Sometimes Aunt Selena would come out the front door and say, "Would you like to take a bunch home, Gwennie?" I would nod, speechless. She would understand, knowing how much I loved them.

Living as we did with our front verandah over the water and a steep hill at the back of the house, we had no space for a flower garden. We kept nasturtiums and pansies in boxes on the verandah and our windowsills were bedecked with begonias, fuchsias, and geraniums tenderly nurtured by my mother.

Continuing down the "route," we pass the Jameses, the Anthonys, the Lockes, the Ryans, the Cobbs, and the Chappells. My grandfather's brother Jesse, of whom my father was a namesake, had a house at the bottom of the lane where Harold

Warr's house later stood. Uncle Jesse had a brood of young ones. There was Lush, Llewellyn, Freda, Winnie, and Leo. I've forgotten the others.

Opposite the lane from Uncle Jesse's house was another family of Ryans (Aunt Blanche lived on that very spot many years later), then the Browns. Their house was adjacent to the "tide." I remember Uncle Neddy Brown mostly because of the fact that he had a very large mouth and because some wag had made a joke about it. It took the form of a poem about one of the numerous delays of the coastal boat, the *Clyde,* and went like this:

"She'll soon be here," said Eleazar Weir,
"I heard her blow," said old John Snow,
"She's stuck in the 'Tide,'" said Harry Boyd,
"She's hard aground," said Neddy Brown.
He opened his mouth and swallowed her down.

At the top of the hill lived Aunt Jessie Harris, presumably a widow, and I couldn't remember any Uncle Harris ever. She was childless and alone. Frequently she would invite me in, sit me down in the antique rocker with the velvet pillow sham, and leave me with a glass of goat's milk and a slice of her delicious gingerbread while she went outside to cut me an armful of her plump, red rhubarb. It would be the highlight of my day.

Coming home from school we often took a shortcut, down Harris's Hill, a rocky slope that required some manipulation, and great glee when we reached the bottom. At the bottom of the hill lived Arthur Rendall, his wife, and adopted daughter Ivy.

After crossing the bar the first house to pass on our final leg home was that of Uncle Phil and Aunt Susie Vineham. Aunt Susie and Uncle Phil were a unique pair, and worthy of some comment. Aunt Susie was my Sunday school teacher. If she couldn't pronounce the words, she would look to me for prompting. Aunt Susie was also the cleanest person I had ever met, or ever met since, for that matter. She had two kitchens, and an outside porch where Uncle Phil discarded his dirty boots, then proceeded to the first kitchen for his mug of tea. On special occasions he was allowed in the second kitchen with its spotless hooked mats, highly polished black wood-burning stove, well-scrubbed tables and chairs, eight-day clock ticking merrily in the corner, and a sideboard with the most extraordinary arrangement of china and glassware that would have delighted the eyes of my antique collector daughter, Gail, and niece Janice today.

I stopped by weekly for an exchange of books Aunt Susie had gotten from the old hospital library when it was disbanded. Uncle Phil had worked there as custodian. After making sure that I had wiped my feet very carefully in all three outer rooms, I was allowed into the "holy of holies," a front room that today would be even more of an antique dealer's dream than the second kitchen. There stood her old-fashioned organ, overflowing with pictures of Vinehams past and present, ancient tables loaded with odds and ends of another century, squeaky-clean mats hooked with white background and splashy red roses and green leaves done in a magnificent scrollwork. The floral wallpaper was a good background for the old-fashioned oval-framed pictures of Vineham ancestors, interspersed with samplers, one of which read "God Bless our Home."

In one corner stood a huge bookcase designed by Uncle Phil and loaded with books. There Aunt Susie would leave me, in a complete abandonment of joy, while I carefully and reverently searched until I found what I wanted. I suspect that the older Vinehams rarely dipped into those books, but Aunt Susie cherished them as lending an air of distinction to her best parlour.

The Vinehams had one son, Stanley, married to Flossie and father of Maisie. They lived with Aunt Susie and Uncle Phil and fitted in nicely, as both Flossie and Maisie were as meticulously clean as was Aunt Susie. Long after the death of his parents, Stanley and family moved away. The house was purchased by cousin Ed (by then a lawyer living in Corner Brook), as a summer home, and was dubbed Stanleyville. Ed and Cyril (then a university academic) kept their boats, the *Shamrock II* and *Primrose III*, there. The original *Shamrock* and

Primrose were owned by Grandfather Poole in Sop's Arm. Together with their brother Winston, and my brother Don, they spent many long, lazy holidays at Stanleyville. Both in the house and in their boats they entertained a great number and striking variety of people, from Newfoundland, several other provinces, and the West Country of England, including members of the British Peerage. Shades of Aunt Susie!

The next house was that of Aunt Selena Blackmore. Her daughter Alma married Albert Payne, brother to Ned, who married cousin Una. Then, a family of Ryans lived where Una's house is now, and then Uncle George Ledrew, who always seemed to be sawing wood as Madge and I skipped past on our way home from school. He never failed to greet us with "another day punched in," until we came to expect it day after day.

Next to the Ledrews lived Uncle Billy Witt, whose goat was famous for giving phenomenal amounts of milk. On days when our goats didn't come home, or if we needed extra milk, Mom would send one of us, usually Madge, in to Billy's with a five-cent piece for a pint of milk. Uncle Billy's pipe was so permanently stuck in his mouth that we wondered if he removed it when he slept.

Next to Uncle Billy's lived the Blackmores, a rowdy bunch. Max was the school bully and fought the other boys (and girls) on the least provocation. Sister Gladys especially became the target of his ire on the way home from school. Gladys's intelligence, and her lofty way of looking down her nose at him with an air of disdain and scorn, really got to Max. As Gladys was small and unused to brawling, I don't know what the outcome might have been had it not been for our formidable sister, Geneva, who never ran away from a fight. With fists flailing she put the boys, one by one, to flight. I stayed under her wing, for the most part, and escaped the enemy.

The next house belonged to Pierce and Margaret Blackmore, distant cousin to Max. It nestled in a hollow at the foot of a wide, sweeping meadow with an apple tree in front. I have a very dim recollection of Pierce's parents, who both met tragic deaths. His father committed suicide, and his mother – Aunt Betsy – died suddenly. My grandmother, her good friend, found her body early one morning. Grandma had gone to the well for a "turn" of water, the well being on Blackmore's property. She decided to call on Aunt Betsy and found her dead by the kitchen stove. She had been in the act of lighting the morning fire, a match in one hand, and birch rind kindling in the other. Fortunately for her children, Pierce and Lily, asleep upstairs, she hadn't applied the match.

Soon after, Lily married Harold Warr. Harold's father had started a combination hardware, grocery and dry goods store in Springdale, about two hours away by motorboat, called George Warr & Sons, with a branch in Pilley's Island which Harold inherited. It became a thriving business, outfitting men for the fisheries on the French Shore and Labrador, and supplying most of the Island folk.

Pierce Blackmore married Margaret Scott of Twillingate, who deserves a dossier all her own. Margaret Scott graduated from St. John's General Hospital School of Nursing and came to Pilley's Island to work in the "mine hospital." In those early years of the twentieth century, iron ore and pyrites were being mined in Pilley's Island. For a time it was prosperous and thriving, but was of short duration. In the meantime, Margaret met and married Pierce Blackmore, who also had a general store. Margaret became the undisputed leader of Pilley's Island society, vying with Ivy Curtis for that dubious honour. Margaret's reign lasted for nigh unto forty years, and in later years they bought Anstey's house by the government wharf, which to our untutored eyes was even more palatial than the white house by the well.

We were all in awe of Mrs. Blackmore with her superior airs and her general bossiness. She was the only nurse on the Island, and naturally she wasn't always right, as my mother was soon to discover.

Proceeding around the shore, the next house belonged to Flossie and Cliff Oxford, the same house in which my early friend Ada Rideout had lived. Flossie and Cliff were kind, good people and congenial neighbours. They had four young daughters, one my sister Madge's age, and two sons.

Next, a small house sheltered Flossie's father, Uncle Amaziah Guy, and her brother Cammie. Uncle Amaziah was a jolly man, with a big laugh and belly equally big. Cammie was a long-time friend. He had a back deformity from birth, but that only seemed to add to his kindliness and charm. He later became a Pentecostal preacher.

Then we were home, Uncle Dorm's house first and then ours, with the back into the steep hill and the front built out over the water and surrounded on three sides by a narrow verandah supported by a breastwork of large logs.

Next a trail takes us to Gowdy's Cove, or more commonly known as "Lorabatt's Cove." Inaccessible cliffs, jutting out into the harbour, prevented the road going any farther. Up in "the bottom" lived a family of Ryans with a gaggle of kids who appeared to be much worse off than we were. I can't remember all their names, but one of them named Ronald, and nicknamed "Wad" for some obscure reason, was always getting into trouble. Accident-prone as he was, one winter almost saw the early demise of Wad. A snowslide fell suddenly where the children had been playing seconds earlier. All the children were accounted for except Wad. A general alert sounded to all and sundry. It was my mother who finally rescued Wad.

Digging furiously in the snow with her mittened hands, she heard a feeble mewl. Renewing her efforts, she came in contact with a rubber boot. Luckily for Wad, he was wearing his father's boots, too big, and they formed a pocket of air, and soon Wad was pulled out, blue and shivering and scared, but none the worse for the experience. My mother was a heroine for a day or two, until the hubbub died down, and another crisis arose.

The Ryans' grandfather, Uncle Billy, had a tiny notions shop. He sold things like tobacco, spools of thread, shoelaces, candy, and gum. When I went there with my mother for one of her purchases, Uncle Billy would offer me a peppermint knob in exchange for a kiss. I must have been around five, then, and I was so entranced at the offer of candy that I would have kissed the devil himself. I was revolted by his tobacco whiskers, but the kiss was soon over, and the candy lasted much longer.

Next to the Ryans lived Alf and Clara Ward, with children whose names I've forgotten. "Poor Clara," as she was always referred to by my mother, had been a childhood friend of hers in Leading Tickles, where they had both grown up. Although we were poor, "Poor Clara" was even poorer, and Mom helped her out in any way she could. Clara was very proud and always insisted on repaying favours. I can remember her scrubbing our back porch on her hands and knees in exchange for some rabbit soup, or handmade gloves and socks, or for a few cakes of homemade lye soap. Eventually they moved, I think back to Leading Tickles.

Next, a family of Fudges; how or whence they came, or whither they went, I do not know. I just remember they were there. A bit farther up in the very bottom of the cove lived Aunt Nora and Uncle Billy Ward. They had two daughters, Fanny and Mary, and two sons, Charlie and Douglas, the latter of whom was Geneva's age.

The elder son, Charlie, met a tragic end. He was returning from Pretty Island with a load of wood when he swamped his punt. Months later, my cousins Roy and Cyril discovered his body washed up on a beach. The boys returned home in a state of shock. Always a stutterer, at time of stress Roy could scarcely speak at all. White as a ghost, with eyes popping and shivering uncontrollably, he managed to stutter out the story to his father and mine while we children stood aghast. It was weeks before Roy returned to a semblance of his former self.

Aunt Nora Ward visited our house a lot. Sometimes Uncle Billy dropped her off in his rowboat, but more often than not she came striding over the hills, her long petticoats flapping against her high button-up boots. My mother was unwell and depressed for months after brother Don's birth, and she was glad to have Aunt Nora lend her a hand. She helped take care of us kids and do the housework. Her treatment of us was not intentionally rough, but when she got at the tangles in my hair she had no mercy, and when she washed me, my arms practically bled from her scrubbing. All the while she kept up a ceaseless monotone of complaints about Uncle Billy, who "was too unhandy to crawl up under the house!" Poor Uncle Billy didn't stand a chance with Aunt Nora.

In later years Aunt Nora became almost fanatically religious. She had attended the Salvation Army, as did most of the people, but then a couple of roving evangelists on a quest of converting souls to their faith landed on the Island, and Aunt Nora became their staunch adherent. Mr. Law and Mr. Price would gather a few people together in any empty storefront or back shed or whatever, and Aunt Nora attended faithfully. They came for two or three consecutive years, staying at Aunt Nora's and preaching to anyone who would listen. They finally stopped coming, whether from a lack of audience or Aunt Nora's cooking was the wag's question.

Leaving Aunt Nora's and proceeding up a steep hill, we eventually came to the Tizzards, who lived in a house on a point of land known as Tizzard's Point. I remember they had two daughters, much older than I. They were still living there when I left home, but the family and house itself are long since gone.

Then down in the "landwash" lived Uncle Ned and Aunt Mary Payne. They were parents of Carrie,

Emmeline, Blanche, Madeline, Albert, and Ned, who later became husband to cousin Una. We often rowed out to Aunt Mary's. She was such a friendly soul, and I loved most of all to look at pictures through her stereoscope. I thought it was just the greatest, and wished we had one like it.

Proceeding along the shady path, slightly back from the waterfront, amid tall trees of birch and spruce, lived the Guys, three families in all, but that goes way back, and my recollection is dim about them. I only know that my father was a good friend of Sophie Guy, meeting her in his later years in Moncton, New Brunswick, and that Uncle Amaziah was the last of the Guys and came to live near us with his daughter Flossie Oxford. The place is known to this day as Guy's Point.

The very last house on that part of the Island belonged to Bertha Metcalfe and her mother. I never heard of a father Metcalfe, so I presume he was long since dead. It was a big, two-storey yellow house overlooking the narrows. I remember it best for their lovely flower garden, with hollyhocks climbing the fence. It was a glorious, untidy mess of flowers running riot, and sometimes as we passed by looking for our goats, Bertha would gather a bouquet for us. Or, sometimes on a Sunday morning, she would row in the harbour, tie up to our wharf, and, passing our house on the way to the Barracks, she would hand my mother a large armful of flowers. In our breakfast room, which had been Grandma Poole's kitchen, we had a table in the middle of the room, covered with a green, fringed tablecloth, and I can still see the old-fashioned pitcher filled with Bertha's blooms and smell the boy's love.

Every day Bertha climbed the hills surrounding her home on the thinnest legs I've ever seen, in search of her wandering goat "Magnificent." On a clear day we could hear her shrill voice echoing and re-echoing across the harbour "Come, Mag-NIF-i-cent, Mag-NIF-i-cent." Bertha, her mother, the house, and Magnificent are long since gone and only a grassy knoll remains. Metcalfe's house was on the farthermost point of the Island, so, in order to describe the remaining inhabitants, we must backtrack to Lorabatt's Cove over the hill, through the marsh, and back over the bar.

Leaving the bar, on the right side was the home of Ches and Lily Boyd. Then, on to the residence of Harold and Lily (Blackmore) Warr, which was more imposing and well-kept than the rest of the houses. Lily was a quiet, introverted woman. It was said she had never gotten over the shock of her parents' death. That, in addition to the fact that both her husband, Harold, and brother, Pierce, drank heavily, gave her the appearance of being haunted and unhappy, and we had little contact with Lily. One day as Madge was running up the hill opposite her house, she slipped and fell, cutting her knee badly. Lily saw her crying, took her in her house, cleansed the knee of blood, mud, and grit, and applied a dressing, all with the utmost kindness. After that she had a special place in our hearts and we came to know that she was a very kind and compassionate woman.

At the top of the hill was George Warr's store. It wasn't very imposing but housed every imaginable household need. Later on, the son, Harold, built a larger store farther up the road. I can barely remember Aunt Mary Ann Warr. She was my grandmother's friend, a tall, formidable-looking woman with masses of white hair piled high on her head, with a comb in the back. She had the reputation, deserved or not, of being a penny-pincher. Perhaps her frugality rubbed off a bit on her son. In later years, when I worked in his store, I found him to be a no-nonsense businessman, except for the times when he locked himself in his office and quietly drank. I, at seventeen, was left to deal with the men being outfitted for the Labrador fishery, balancing the books, and waiting on all and sundry, a feat which I accomplished with remarkable aplomb considering my age and lack of experience.

A bit farther up the road was the general store of Mark Winsor. Mark was a bit of a rogue, but so merry that he was universally liked. I think I may have been eight when Mark pulled up stakes, took himself a young wife, and departed for California. Upon Mark's departure, Pierce Blackmore took over his store. It was quite large, with a pot-bellied stove in the middle and shelves and counters on either side. On the left were stacked canned goods, staples of all kinds, and on the counter a huge cheese that was cut on demand and carefully weighed in the scales hanging above.

On the opposite side dry goods made a colourful showing. As all our clothes were made by my mother from the bolts of cloth on the shelves, they made quite a fascinating mixture. My mother would finger the shirting, the sheeting, the serge and flannelette, as well as the dress crinkle crepes and cottons, long and painstakingly, and carefully watched the cutting of the yardage to make sure she got her money's worth while I watched impatiently, keeping an eye on the candy jars, hoping to get at least a chocolate man!

Pierce Blackmore had a warehouse underneath the hill, by the water's edge, and here he stored the tubs of butter, barrels of flour, bags of sugar, kegs of molasses, huge barrels of salt beef and pork, bags of rice, dried beans and peas, and all the other essentials to feed the Island's inhabitants and to outfit the schooners that left in the spring for the summer fishery on the French Shore or Labrador Coast. The supplies were replenished weekly by the coastal steamer, but extras had to be laid in for the time when navigation closed. Every fall my father would gather in enough supplies to hopefully last us throughout the winter. He had one of Pierce Blackmore's little black books in which everything was charged. The debit account on the left side, as opposed to the offerings of fish, lumber, canned rabbits, moose, lobster, salmon, mussels, and bakeapples deposited to his credit. Weekly, one of us had to balance his book which usually ended up in the red.

On Saturday nights Pierce Blackmore's store was the men's gathering place. It was the Island's closest thing to a clubhouse, and there they would discuss the week's happenings, their salmon nets, their lobster pots, and their quintals of dried fish. They would also expound at great length on politics, religion, and any and every subject. My father was one of the acknowledged orators, and his views and ideas were seriously discussed and considered by his cronies. "If Jesse Poole said it, it must be so."

To the right of the store, a road ran parallel to the waterfront. On the left was the Salvation Army Quarters. I was a regular visitor there as the officer's daughter, Etta Pike, was a special friend of mine when we were both about ten. Under the hill lived the Colbournes and the Ginns, while up another hill lived the Hacketts. On the right was the government wharf where the steamers tied up, and to the right of the wharf lived the Ansteys, the Simmses, the Gileses, and the Paynes. After passing Pierce Blackmore's store going east Pete Rowsell lived on the right with his large family.

Peter was a blind organ tuner who kept the residents' organs in tune, including ours. My father played by ear, beautifully, and on Sunday mornings he could be heard all across the harbour, playing and singing his favorite hymns. Peter kept our organ well-tuned.

Next to Peter Rowsell's stood a small, one-room building, grandly dubbed the Courthouse. It was famous more for the square dance parties held there than for legal matters. The Island was singularly free of crime. Few people ever broke the law or stepped out of line. We had no policemen or lawmen. I remember one occasion when a Justice of the Peace came from nearby Little Bay and presided over a court trial of two youthful poachers. They were let off with a severe reprimand.

The United Church stood on a knoll to the right of the Courthouse, quite imposing to our childish eyes. It had a bell tower, and the bell tolled faithfully on Sundays at 11:00 a.m. and again at 7 p.m. The services were always well-attended. Ivy Curtis was the organist and Margaret Blackmore the star soloist.

Across the way from the church was the United Church school, similar to the Salvation Army school, the enrolment fairly evenly distributed. It was a one-room school, housing grades from Primer to Junior Associate. The teacher was always male, single, and young, with the teenage girls swooning helplessly at his feet, but, realizing he was the exclusive property of Miss Curtis, it was hands off and our hero worship kept carefully under wraps.

Not far from the school was the building that was the focal point of all social activities, the Orangemen's Lodge. My father was an Orangeman, and he looked quite important and mysterious on Lodge Nights. He and Uncle Dorm usually went off together, with a lantern to guide their way.

Proceeding along to the right and just before Taylor's Hill was the home of Uncle Will Budgell and Aunt Rachel. He was my mother's uncle, her only relative in Pilley's Island. He was quite a forceful character, emphasizing his words and always ending with "by gummy, by gummy," so it was only natural that we kids called him "Uncle Gummy," behind his back, of course. Aunt Rachel was his second wife. He had children from both wives, but the older ones had left home before he married Aunt Rachel. They had two sons, Harvey and Ford. Aunt Rachel was a kind, sweet woman who was very good to us and always treated us to a glass of her cow's milk when we stopped by at recess time from the nearby school. When she talked she blinked her eyes furiously, which led us to call her "Auntie Blink," and the name stuck forever after, although she was blissfully unconscious of the fact. They had a big, roomy house and itinerant travellers always put up there. It was the closest to a boarding house that Pilley's Island could produce.

Aunt Rachel had a picture in an oval frame in her best parlour. The photographer held transient residence at Aunt Rachel's, and this picture was of my two older sisters and me. I was eight months old, seated in a rocking chair, with Gladys and Geneva on either side of me. Gladys was five, Geneva three and a half. They both wore white muslin dresses, with wide pink sashes and black stockings, and button-up high black boots. The picture wasn't flattering to any of us. My crossed eye was very evident and my sisters were squinting in the sun. When my mother saw the picture, she refused to buy it and so the photographer left in high dudgeon, the picture abandoned to find a resting place in Aunt Rachel's parlour. I liked it, and Aunt Rachel told me it would be mine whenever I wanted to claim it, which I did years later.

Uncle Gummy's house was at the top of Taylor's Hill. Underneath the hill and along the waterfront lived the Tizzards. Their daughter, Gertie, was my good friend, along with Winnie Rideout. We were in the same grade at school and shared a desk. Next to the Tizzards lived the Simmses, and the Verges. Bob Verge was one of the pillars of the community and a Justice of the Peace. Their daughter, Ella, chummed around with my sister Gladys, eventually marrying Nathan Ryan, son of the same Aunt Polly who gave us kids such a hard time when we encroached on her property.

After the Simmses and Verges lived the Moores and the Gileses. Uncle Jim Giles was one of the Island's most colourful characters. He was very vocal in the Saturday night sessions around the pot-bellied stove in Pierce Blackmore's store. His stories often somewhat stretched the truth and were a source of great merriment to Pop and the others.

Then, going northward around the shore in the opposite direction, we pass Mike Whelan's general store. Mike's store was a favourite with my mother, because usually items were a penny or two cheaper there. So, with me tagging along, she would brave the pipe-smoking hangers-on, the store blue with tobacco smoke, and the hit-or-miss spittoons by the pot-bellied stove. Mike was a tobacco-chewing, swarthy, blue-eyed rogue of an Irishman, so genial that he was liked by everybody. He treated my mother with great courtesy, standing patiently by while she fingered the goods and took forever to make up her mind. He would wink at me and, with great ceremony, present me with a chocolate man. After her purchases, the dry goods measured and cut, with perhaps a pound of bulk cheese on the counter, carefully weighed, my mother would lift her skirts and daintily pick her way over the litter of burnt-out matches, cigarette butts, and wads of chewed tobacco, to the door that was held open by

Mike, who ushered us out with a courtly bow and a "good day, ma'am" to my mother and a tug of my pigtails for me.

After leaving Mike Whelan's store, the road stretches a short way along the waterfront. But before continuing on that route, to the left a rather steep hill takes one farther inland. On the top of the hill, known as Curtis's Hill, were two large, imposing houses. The first, a grey, weather-beaten but charming house with large bay windows, wide verandah, and adorned with curlicues, was the home of Ivy Curtis, the postmistress, and her mother.

Miss Curtis was what we then called an old maid. She lived with her mother in the largest, poshest house on the Island, simply loaded with antiquated furniture, and, with Margaret Blackmore, was one of two social leaders of Pilley's Island. We were greatly in awe of Miss Curtis, and heaven help the person who dared to call her Ivy. She had an awesome presence and must have weighed close to three hundred pounds. Her face was mottled and pockmarked, and her voice rasped like the sound of my father filing his bucksaw. Her place in society was firmly entrenched by the fact that she boarded the United Church minister and teacher. They were always young, single men and Ivy soon made known to all and sundry that they were her exclusive property, and woe betide the foolhardy soul who dared poach.

Her father was long since deceased. Her mother was an elegant, cultured lady who reminded me greatly of Queen Alexandra. Her masses of snowy hair, piled high with combs, her patrician face and regal carriage were quite intimidating to me, as weekly I stopped by to borrow books. They had a large library filled with books of all descriptions and a source of great joy to my mother, my sisters, and me, who all shared catholic tastes in literature from the classics, poetry, biographies, history, and fiction of such authors as the Bronte sisters, Louisa May Alcott, P. C. Wren, James Oliver Curwood, Horatio Alger, and a host of others. Miss Curtis was quite generous in the lending of books. I was a sort of protege and I think she enjoyed encouraging my love of books and providing me with the mental stimulus to absorb them.

When I was much older and working as a clerk in Pierce Blackmore's store, the Curtis house was burned to the ground. I closed the store and raced to the fire. Firemen with fire trucks were unheard of, and the people formed a bucket brigade. With the fearlessness of youth, I entered the burning house and, through an upstairs window, I flung out loads of Ivy's dresses, eagerly rescued by people standing below – a veritable flurry of silks, satins, and furs. I was given the credit of salvaging her wardrobe and became the heroine of the hour, despite the fact that I hadn't even stopped to lock the shop door behind me. Fortunately all my potential customers were at the fire and the unlocked door went undetected.

The fire that destroyed the Curtis home also spread to the house nearby, home of the Shearings. Mr. Shearing had been an executive of the mine company and was now retired. He had courtly manners and a very impressive goatee. As a hobby, more or less, he maintained a small variety shop situated below the hill and away from the scene of the fire. My mother always said that Mr. Shearing was the epitome of an old English country gentleman, perhaps because he always kissed her hand when they met. After the fire the Shearings moved away to live with a married daughter.

We frequently took the scenic path from the Curtises' home farther inland to Cobb's Pond. On the left hand was the abandoned cottage hospital, previously owned and operated by the mine. The hospital housed about twenty beds. The doctor was a Dr. Robert Reid Rafter. It was rumoured that he was a drug addict. The head nurse was a Miss Nichols from Buffalo, New York. To my childish fancy, she was a being from another planet, so remote did Buffalo, New York, seem to me then. I don't remember any others except Margaret Scott, later Mrs. Pierce Blackmore.

Opposite the old hospital was a small Roman Catholic chapel, seldom used as there was but a handful of Catholics on the Island. Occasionally a priest would stop by in his motorboat on a Sunday morning and a sprinkling of Catholics would gather for Mass. Next door to the chapel lived Paddy Keating, who was the caretaker. In those days we also regarded Catholics as beings of a world apart. In fact, we knew so little about them that we held them in superstitious awe. The door of the chapel was never locked, and we sometimes ventured in, with great trepidation, standing timidly by the door, poised for instant flight if necessary. Cousin Roy, the leader of the pack, once ventured as far as the altar and gazed in wonderment at the statues and at, what seemed to us, most elaborate fixtures, adorned with intricately stitched cloths, gold embossed tankards, and vials of holy water. Quite without reason, we always raced away from the place as if pursued by a thousand demons.

Farther along, still going inland, was the home of the Cobb family. My most vivid memory of the Cobbs was that they had two daughters in the States who were evidently very prosperous, as they sent bales of clothes home with the result that the remaining daughter, Mabel, was the best-dressed girl on the Island. In fact, later on, when I was a maid of honour for cousin Una, I borrowed a lovely gown from Mabel and felt elegant and poised for the first time in my life. There was also a granddaughter, Doris, who was to play a role in my life in later years.

The road ended at Cobb's Pond, beyond which lay a vast expanse of wild, uncultivated marshland and hills abounding with partridgeberries and blueberries. I have happy memories of our many safaris there. Backtracking to the waterfront and following the road to Bumble Bee Bight, we now pass the abandoned mine territory which covered a large area.

I remember nothing about the mining activity, as it phased out before I was born, but I do recall the library, which was quite extensive. When I was about ten or so, the abandoned hospital became the focus of our ramblings. It seemed a place of mystery, tenanted by the ghosts of the past. I have an early memory of standing on our verandah in the dusk of an evening and watching a huge Norwegian ship coming in the narrows. We could hear the sailors chattering away in their foreign dialect, and we felt we were being invaded. That night, for the first time in my memory, my mother locked and bolted the doors.[2]

The abandoned mines soon became overgrown with blueberry bushes. Some of the happiest memories of my childhood are associated with blueberry picking on the mines. I loved to go on berry picking expeditions with Aunt Blanche – we were pretty

2 - Mining began on Pilley's Island in the late 1880s and ceased production in 1908. The mine was sold for the last time in 1918. The foreign ship in Gwen's memory may have been toward the end of the war, loading machinery which had been sold for scrap metal.

good pals, climbing the hills in the evenings, looking for our goats, as well as our berry picking excursions together. She was witty and entertaining and so much fun.

Along that route was the site of the old post office. This was later abandoned in favour of the more modern one in a building shared with the courthouse. In my mind's eye, I can still see the mailmen with the bags on their backs, sweating from their trek all the way uphill from the boat, down Taylor's Hill and along the shore to the post office. It must have been a great relief to them when the post office was situated closer to the government wharf. I can also see Ivy Curtis, standing in the narrow aperture, doling out the mail. There were a few private mailboxes along the wall and a bench by the door for the patient populace. On the wall was a picture of a dog and, underneath it, the caption:

On the floor a dog wouldn't spit,
He wouldn't, he couldn't;
And people who know more than dogs,
They shouldn't, they shouldn't.

Proceeding on toward Bumble Bee Bight, on the right was the home of Marty Mullins and her parents. Marty was one of the most congenial souls I knew. Everyone liked Marty and ribbed her in a good-natured way. What makes Marty stand out in my mind was the fox fur that she wore to the Barracks every Sunday, winter and summer. Our summers were very hot in those long-ago days and, while I sat there sweating in my middy blouse and skirt, I stared in utter fascination at Marty flouncing in with that red fox fur dangling over her shoulders.

Next was the home of Mike and Melene Whalen, with two sons, Billy and Ches. Melene was a friendly extrovert and, in my teenage years, Whalen's was the gathering place of many of my peers. Melene would cook a boiled dinner consisting of salt beef, cabbage, potatoes, turnips, and carrots, and the traditional pease pudding, all accompanied by homemade rhubarb pickles and beets. After dinner we would play a game of forty-fives way into the morning, Geneva and I always together, Gladys by now having left home and Madge still too young. We kept up the practice and, as Madge grew older, she, too, was included in our get-togethers.

Then there were the homes of the Elliotts, the aforementioned Fifields, Sticklands, Hewletts, and Kings. Then on to the nethermost part of the Bight, where the old abandoned ship, the *Greyhound*, kept silent watch and stands sentinel still.

Masters of Trades

My father and Uncle Dorm made their livelihoods in joint enterprises from lobster canning to sawmilling to the fur trade and would have been lost without each other.

In addition to the family rowboats we children used, each had a small motorboat and jointly owned a much larger one. They took the larger boat to their lobster traps and salmon nets, and to their sawmill at Huzzy's Cove, from which, on their return, they would be loaded down to the gunwales with slabs and lumber.

The sawmill at Hussey's Cove was about forty-five minutes away by motorboat, but I remember rowing there a few times with my father. He would take the forward paddles and I would row back aft. One day, there was a strong wind blowing and, a bit nervous, I rowed like mad, until my father said cheerfully, "The wind is with us, child, don't kill yourself." I relaxed a bit but was relieved when we finally arrived in safe harbour.

Una and I loved to go with our dads to the sawmill. They had a rough shack for overnight stays and we played at keeping house, tidying up the bunks, sweeping the rough wooden floor with a rush broom, and cleaning off the top of the oil drum that served as a stove. Then we watched as they let up the boom; the logs came pouring out and were hauled up to the mill on a conveyor belt. It was fascinating to see how the saw first peeled the slabs off the sides of the logs before converting them into lumber.

We used to get the most violent thunderstorms, and, living under a hill, they seemed to reverberate all the more. I was terrified as a small child and would hide in the pantry under the stairs. My mother could tell when a storm was way off and would herd us children out on the flake when the quintals of codfish were drying in the sun. We would gather them in neat stacks or "yaffles," as they were called, and quickly cover them with wooden "faggots," small cone-like structures made for the purpose of securing them from the weather.

Sometimes in the late evening when the men were due home from the mill or lobster factory in Badger Bay in the midst of a thunderstorm, I would go in the front room that overlooked the water and strain for the sound of a familiar motor. It had a cadence all its own and we could distinguish it out beyond Payne's Island before it ever appeared in the narrows. Our mongrel dog Buddy would also recognize the sound of the motor and be out on the wharf, jumping and barking as they tied up.

I didn't mind any of the chores we had to do for our fathers, as long as both families did them together. We would help clean the bakeapples, pick out the mussels, label the tins, and spread the codfish to dry. As a concerted effort, we enjoyed it. Another two-family effort was the spreading of caplin on the flakes. A caplin is a small silvery fish resembling smelt. It would take at least five roasted caplin to make me a meal. Flakes were built over the water, constructed of small logs, a few inches apart for the purpose of air circulation, and then covered with evergreen boughs. On the boughs, we painstakingly laid the caplin head to tail in a neat row to dry in the sun.

We associated the caplin season with exam writing time, as they always appeared in mid-June. They came in shoals and the men had no problem filling their boats. They would cast their nets in any of the surrounding beaches and reap the harvest. In fact, I once helped my father cast caplin over our front verandah.

We would come home from writing our final exams and there would be fresh caplin sizzling in the pan. The dried caplin would be stored for the coming winter when many a breakfast would be enhanced by the smell and taste of this tasty, though rather pungent, bill of fare. The remainder of the caplin would be toted laboriously up the hill to fertilize the potatoes, turnips, carrots, and cabbages.

Vegetables were stored for winter use in the outside cellars, dug into the ground and sodded all around and on top. To obtain entrance to the cellar, we had to descend a short ladder. To reach the bins situated on either side we had to venture into the gloomy, nethermost regions. It was creepy, crawly, and Madge, usually so complacent and submissive, absolutely refused to go down the cellar. She declared she was afraid of the earwigs, wiggly insects with multiple legs. We had always heard (though erroneously) that they entered the human ear, and so poor Madge was terrified of them. I, being a little braver, elected to play martyr.

Occasionally, Pop and Uncle Dorm would bundle both families in the big motorboat for an overnight stay in Badger Bay about a three-hour motor away to pick bakeapples. This berry is indigenous to that area. Why they were called bakeapples was a mystery to us as they were small berries, yellow when ripe and totally delicious. They grew on bogs and the hike in the heat and mosquitoes from the waterfront to the bogs left us wilted and drained of the high spirits with which we had started. However, when we saw the bogs alive with yellow, we fell to in earnest and, among us all, occasionally picked enough for commercial canning.

At night we camped on the beach, our arms and necks dripping mosquito repellent. Pop and Uncle Dorm would cook mussels and feed us homemade bread, pork buns, and bangbellies out of their breadboxes. A breadbox was a large wooden tub, with a rope across the top for carrying. They had been sanded and painted and could carry quite a store of food.

In a festive mood, our fathers would tell stories and sing songs, and Uncle Dorm would do his own little special dance while the moon hung low over the water until, tired and sunburnt and happy, we crawled under the big tent and into oblivion.

Upon arriving home our job was to clean the bakeapples, after which the men put them in pound tins, reamed them, put on labels marked "Packed by Dorman Poole" or "Poole Brothers," and stacked them in cases of twenty-four, after which they were shipped to Canada and England. This, though, was a small and sporadic enterprise compared to the cases of lobster that were also packed, labelled, and shipped off to exporters in St. John's and then on to the tables of England.

During the fall we picked squashberries and partridgeberries. Squashberries grew on taller trees, but the partridgeberries – much like cranberries – grew low on the ground. We had to go to outlying coves and islands to obtain enough of both to last throughout the winter. Once, while picking partridgeberries with Pop, I had wandered away a bit and found myself under a steep hill, while he was higher up on level ground. I happened to glance around and saw steaming hot but chilling evidence of where a bear had very recently been. Sir Edmund Hillary would have been proud of the way I scaled that hill.

The densely wooded country adjacent to Pilley's Island, reached only by boat or dog team, was a mecca for trappers. In the fall my father and Uncle Dorm trapped lynx, otter, beaver, red fox, silver fox, cross-patch fox, muskrat, and weasel. At the end of a two-week safari, they would return with the spoils. We liked to guess just how many fox, etc. had been trapped and we could always tell by the look on my father's face if they had been successful. I remember one year when a visiting fur trader bought all their furs accumulated over months. They received the grand sum of six hundred dollars, divided equally – three hundred dollars! We were rich! My father gave us each a little spending money. My share was fifty cents! What a fortune! I racked my brains as to the disposal thereof and finally sent away for an Elsie Dinsmore book. What fifty cents could purchase in those days!

Bears were exceedingly rare on our island, but one day just after we finished supper, Geneva went out on the front verandah and came racing back yelling to Pop that a bear was up on the hill. He grabbed his rifle and shouted next door to Uncle Dorm for reinforcements. Uncle Dorm ran, carrying his shotgun, which unfortunately was empty. However, Pop downed the bear with two shots, and it rolled over and over down the hill, landing on the beach. People came from all over to see the bear, which had evidently swum over from the mainland, and some of them took meat to eat, but none of my family would ever touch bear meat. We did, however, keep the bear skin as a rug.

Uncle Dorm was usually pretty quick. I remember Pop chuckling one day after he and Dorm had been casting caplin. As Uncle Dorm threw out the net, one part of it held between his teeth, his dentures were about to accompany the net into the foaming sea. With great presence of mind, Uncle Dorm plunged his hand in the water and rescued his teeth just as they were disappearing.

Una and I learned a lot about our fathers' enterprises. Occasionally we went with them when they hauled their lobster pots. Each pot had a buoy marker and it was thrilling to see the pot emerge with a huge lobster inside.

Sometimes our fathers went on overnight stays at Sop's Arm, where the family lived before moving to Pilley's Island in 1904. It was now deserted, save for wide meadows of tall grass which they would cut with their long scythes, raking it into bundles to take home for the horse and goats in the coming winter. We children were sometimes granted the treat of going along on the two-hour boat ride. On the return trip in the quiet dusk of the evening, with the moon rising over the mountaintops reflected in the clear waters of the bay, we would sit on the sweet-smelling hay and sing, mostly hymns, all the way home. Sometimes Pop and Uncle Dorm, who both had great singing voices, would join us and our blended voices would float over the water, keeping time with the cadence of the waves lapping softly on the opposite shore. Such a time of peace and togetherness, in which, briefly, we had not a care in the world.

The Next Generation

Gladys, born in 1910, was the oldest and the most avid bookworm of us all. She was always on cloud nine and, most of the time, seemed oblivious to her surroundings when immersed in a book. A very bright child of budding promise, she grew up to be the family intellectual, writing poetry and short stories. Later in life she wrote a treatise on roses for *The Canadian Rose Society* that prompted a request to publish by the prestigious British publication *The Rose*.

Geneva, born one year later, was also a brainy child but, in other aspects, they were totally unalike and frequently at loggerheads. They fought and quarrelled and disagreed about most everything. Four years younger than Geneva, I was the self-appointed peacemaker and refereed many a fight. Battling among themselves was one thing, but just let an outsider attack one or the other and they closed ranks fiercely against the intruder, loyally protecting their sibling.

Madge was born when I was five, and how I adored her! I was so proud the first day I led her to school, dressed in a little pink pantsuit and a pink bow in her hair – she was adorable. She looked a lot like Grandma Poole, inheriting her periwinkle blue eyes and her jet-black hair. Christened "Haidee Madge," the first name was soon dropped as so many people couldn't pronounce it. Aunt Kizzie Callahan came to visit and asked my mother why she had called the baby "Eddy Match"; so, from then on, she became our Madge. Madge was a complacent child, sunny and agreeable and, I think, gave our mother the fewest heartaches of us all. She was never so happy as when some of us were telling her fairy tales or spinning some concoctions of our own.

Of that last, Geneva was a champion. After school, accompanied by Madge, she would go upstairs to make the beds. During the bed making periods, she would tell Madge a continuing story – drawn on her imagination – of love and romance and thrilling happenings that seemed so lifelike that Madge couldn't wait for the next day's episode. Doubtless, Geneva appreciated an audience for her imaginative creations, as well as her small sister's company in the semi-dusk of the unlighted upstairs bedrooms. It was nearly 10:30 p.m. before it was clear dark in the summertime. Then we would lie in bed, listening to Geneva's stories, giggling and talking until Mom would call, "Children, not another sound," and we would fall asleep in the undisturbed peace and quiet of the still night, for long hours of sweet, dreamless slumber. In later years, one of Geneva's children, Karen, on the occasion of a visit to Pilley's Island, remarked, "It's so dark I can go to sleep with my eyes open."

I was ten when brother Don made his appearance in the world. My mother, quite pleased to present my father with a boy after having four girls, was quite dumbfounded when he looked taken aback and blurted, "Oh, Millie, I thought 'twould be another girl." However, he soon recovered from the shock, and immediately little Donnie was the centre of the household, the pride and joy of us all. After the birth of my brother, my mother fell into postpartum depression. It was months before she recovered, if indeed she ever recovered. With no medical help, she resorted to Dr. Chase's Nerve Food Pills, taking some thirty boxes to the tune of fifty cents per box. She finally decided to discard them with very little noticeable result.

We all tried our best to help. Gladys, now fifteen, quit school that entire winter, and was a great help with the housework. Geneva and I struggled manfully after school, filling the woodbox, bringing buckets of water with a hoop from Blackmore's well, filling the water barrel in the corner, making the bread (left to rise overnight), emptying the chamber pots, carrying out the slop pail to dump in the outhouse built over the water, and countless other jobs which we hated but performed with great stoicism.

Don was an asthmatic baby and many a night

was spent by the kitchen stove, applying linseed meal poultices. Armed with her huge doctor's book, and with the help of Aunt Blanche, my mother managed to get through the long, cold spring until, during the summer months, both she and my brother improved considerably.

Aunt Blanche had her hands full, with raising five children of her own; Cyril, Winston, Mervyn, Joyce, and Edward (she gave birth to six, but little Dorothy died in infancy), and two stepchildren: Una, who was two years older than I and quite amenable, and Roy, who was a bit of a rebel, very nearly the same age as Geneva. Una and I spent a lot of time together. Roy was always disappearing and much valuable time was expended looking for him. One night, he slept in the barn hayloft and stayed there until boredom and hunger forced him out. Roy was full of tricks and he got us all in scrapes of one kind or another. He spent a lot of time at our house and we enjoyed having him.

Aunt Blanche was fun, loving and gay, a direct contrast to my rather reserved, sober mother. But they were very good friends and had many a chat over a borrowed cup of sugar and long discussions about the children, sitting on each other's verandah in the twilight dusk. Though often at variance on other subjects, on one thing they agreed completely: child discipline. With little time to be indulgent, they were no-nonsense parents and spanking was the rule of the day.

My father and Uncle Dorm were away from home a lot, lobster fishing for a week at a time, hunting, trapping, and logging, staying in one or another of their shacks along the way, often for two weeks at a time. But even when he was at home, my father left all the disciplining to our mother. If we asked her if we could do something or go somewhere and she said "ask your father," we just skipped off, knowing we were home free.

My mother demanded strict obedience. For example, she visited a neighbour one evening and sat each of us on a chair, admonishing us not to move until she came back. She probably wasn't gone for long but, to us, the time seemed endless. When she returned, we were still sitting on the same chairs; we hadn't moved. I suppose in this enlightened day and age, such discipline might be classified as child abuse. However, we in no way resented it; it was a way of life with us and I'm sure we were none the worse for the experience.

In the spring, summer, and fall, catching tomcods, flatfish, and conners over the stage head was also a way of life for us. We would catch a fish, calmly scoop out its eye as bait with our thumbnail, put it on the hook, and resume our fishing.

On winter evenings we sat around the kitchen table doing our homework while Mom knitted in the rocking chair by the stove and, Pop, on the rare evenings when he was in the house and not working at something, snored on the kitchen couch. Somehow the evenings didn't seem complete until we heard a tap on the door which opened to Roy's grinning, sheepish face. Lessons finished, we had a short time for recreation, maybe a game of "click the button" invented by our mother. She had an awesome collection of large, fancy buttons and the object of the game was to see who could flick the button closest to the bottle upended in the middle of the table. It became hilarious and Roy was quite a pro at it. We played checkers, snakes and ladders, dominoes, Flinch and Rook; sometimes we took turns at reciting poetry and memorizing long paragraphs from Shakespeare. Our great love of poetry was nurtured by our mother, who could recite one lengthy poem after another, non-stop. There was such a sense of togetherness between the two families in those long, winter evenings and it remains today, whenever we are able to come together.

Geneva, left and Gwen, 1916.

An early photo of Pilley's Island. Buildings on the ridge to the right include the old United Church School and the Salvation Army Citadel. Among the structures closer to the shoreline are, from left: Roland McGinn's, Warr's store, Warr's fish shop and William Colbourne's. (Photo courtesy of the Green Bay Economic Development Association)

A room in the children's section of the old Pilley's Island hospital. (Photo courtesy of the Green Bay Economic Development Association)

Robert Dudley Alcock, 1929.

Pilley's Island Harbour, circa 1900. (Photo courtesy of the Green Bay Economic Development Association)

Gladys's graduation from Grace Hospital Nurses training, 1936.

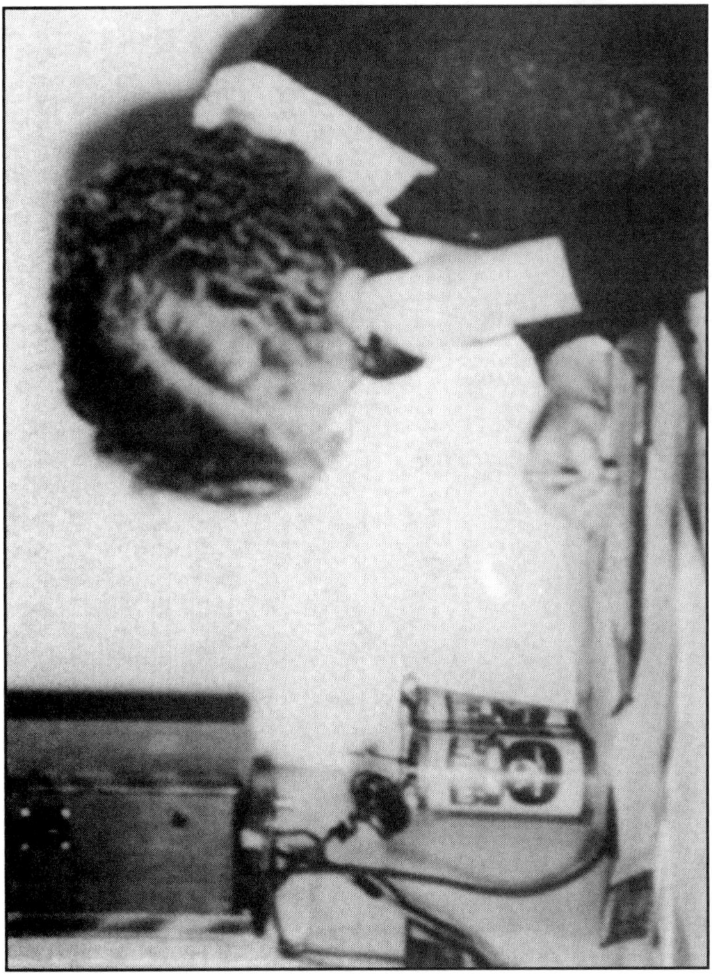

At one time, the only way to send or receive news on Pilley's Island was through mail, transported by dogsled in winter, or by visiting the old telegraph office. (Photo courtesy of the Green Bay Economic Development Association)

Orangemen of Pilley's Island: from left: William Budgell, George Ryan, Harry Boyde and Edward Locke. (Photo courtesy of the Green Bay Economic Development Association)

Lucy Way Poole and daughter Ethel.

Lillian and Ethel Poole, circa 1927.

Lucy Way Poole

The coastal vessel *Nonia* entering port at Pilley's Island. (Photo courtesy of the Green Bay Economic Development Association)

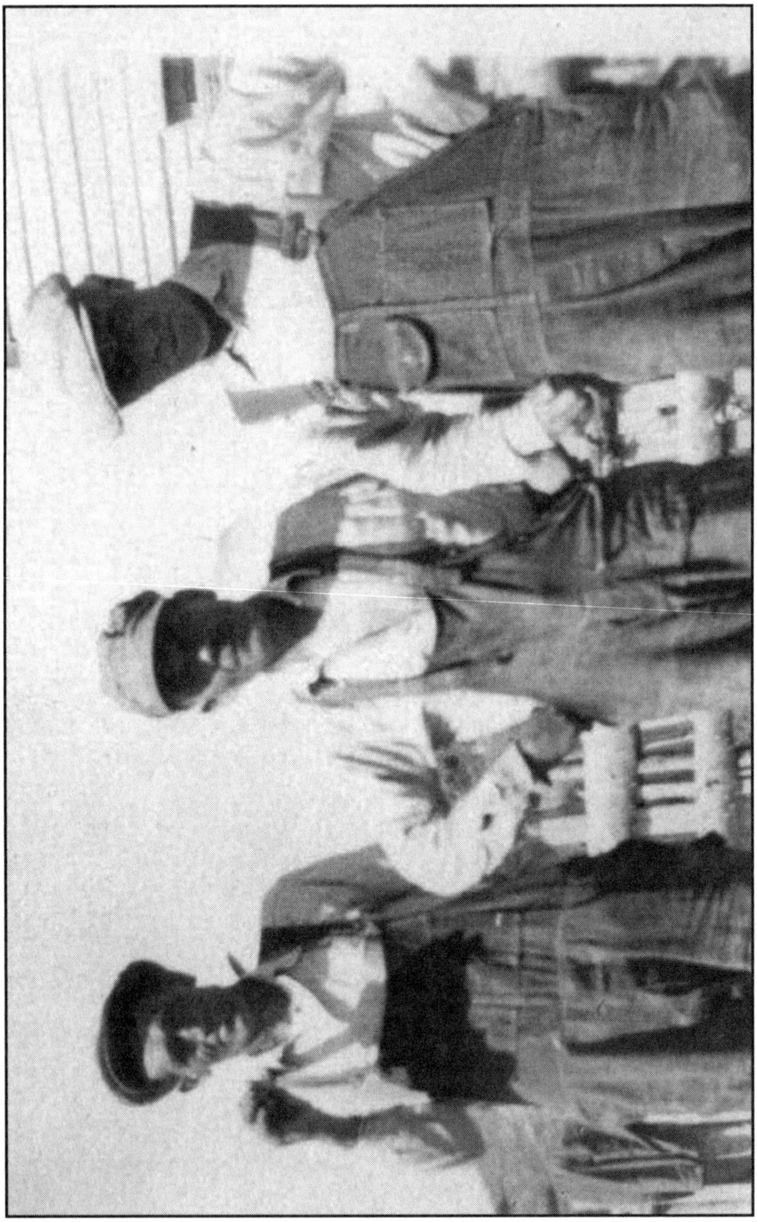

Jesse, centre, with unidentified friends, possibly Albert Weir or George Tizzard on Jesse's right.

Mervyn, Winston, Joyce, Ed and Cyril, in front of Jesse's house, Dorm's behind Cyril, circa 1945.

Don, left, and Cyril, at Lorabatt's Pond, circa 1940.

Don and Jesse, circa 1935.

Ettie Pike, left, and Gwen, circa 1925.

Dougie Ward and Gwen, ready to skate, circa 1927.

Gwen and Don, Lorabatt's Cove.

Geneva, left, and Gwen.

Madge, left and Marge Dinney, circa 1935.

Don and Gwen on front bridge, circa 1935.

Blanche and Gwen, on the front bridge, circa late 1930s.

Gwen in Margaret Blackmore's field, circa 1940.

Gwen

Panoramic view of Pilley's Island Harbour, circa 1945.

Jesse's house and Dorm's separated by barn and woodsheds.

Feeding the Spirit

All the residents of the Island were of British, Scottish, or Irish descent. They were pious, God-fearing people, perhaps fifty percent of them were members of the Methodist (United) Church and the rest belonging to the Salvation Army, with a sprinkling of Roman Catholics. My mother had grown up in Leading Tickles as a staunch Church of Englander, steeped in the religion by her strict old-school father, Robert Dudley Alcock.

However, after her marriage, she attended the Salvation Army with my father, who was the Corps Sergeant Major, complete with uniform. He was hard-working in his faith and lived it on a daily basis. My mother was less vocal than my father in her beliefs, but she spent much time reading her Bible and absorbing religious tracts and spent lengthy periods on her knees, by her bedside, morning and night. We were truly steeped in religious traditions. No day began or ended without prayer, and no meal was eaten without table grace. If, in "after" years, we sometimes strayed, we never forgot the faith of our beginnings.

When I was growing up in outport Newfoundland, the weekend hadn't been invented. There was Saturday night, which was bath night, and Sunday, which was for going to church. No one ever dreamed of accepting an invitation for Saturday night. In fact, no one ever received one, for parties and other forms of social activities on that night were taboo, it being devoted to getting ready for Sunday.

In our home the process really began immediately after the customary Saturday midday dinner of pea soup and dumplings, with steamed pudding and hot molasses for dessert. While our mother did the Saturday baking, we five children had our chores: polishing the flatware, bringing pails of water from the well, and piling high the kitchen woodbox. We gave special attention to the black cast-iron stove. First it received a coat of blacking, and then a lot of elbow grease was expended on the polishing. Nothing but a high shine was satisfactory to my mother. Then the kitchen linoleum was scrubbed on our hands and knees, and finally the old wooden floor of the back porch. What sweat and tears we laboured! After Geneva got the boards whitened to her satisfaction, heaven help the foolhardy souls who dared to track mud across it. Don and Cyril were usually the offenders, calling down a rain of abuse on their heads.

I think the chore I hated most was the weekly ironing. We had four irons that we kept hot on the stove, alternating them as they cooled off. We wore serge skirts and middy blouses for the most part, and cotton pinafores and dresses. Everything had to be ironed according to Mom's rule: no wash-and-wear in those days. Then there were Pop's Sunday serge pants that had to be pressed every Saturday, and Mom's grey gabardine skirts, and white blouses with high necklines. Even our petticoats were scrupulously ironed, and woe betide the culprit who left a wrinkle. After the ironing, we fitted the lamps with kerosene oil, trimmed the wicks, and washed the lamp chimneys to a polished shine. Occasionally we were sent to the store for a supply of ten-cent pieces for Sunday collection. This last was a pleasant task as it gave us a chance to take out the rowboat and row across the harbour to the store on the other side.

Once our chores were finished we could play until teatime, but after tea, life was earnest, and there was no more play for anyone, for then the operation "Sabbath Preparation" really moved into gear.

We sat in the kitchen on Saturday night. At any time the kitchen was very different from its present-day counterpart, but on Saturday night it became a combination of shoeshine parlour, barbershop, beauty parlour, bathing house, and study. It was a veritable hive of industry. All the family shoes were brought out to be cleaned by my father and brother. Then my father would painstakingly hone his old-fashioned razor and shave, while my mother looked over the Sunday clothes for missing buttons or loose hems. Then the large tin bath would be brought in for the smaller ones and placed before the kitchen stove, which earlier had been blackened and polished until it shone in the lamplight's glow. Then out came the Sunday school manual and we learned our lessons for the next day.

Finally, each of us four girls took turns sitting on a stool before the fire, for our mother to braid our hair so it would be nice and frizzy for Sunday, while she recited poetry. I can still remember those poems – long, narrative, and rather tragic they were, for the most part. As she finished one, we would beg for another, and as her repertoire was seemingly endless, she would oblige until we could no longer ignore the fact that it was bedtime, and off we'd go in our long white nightgowns, sometimes each with an apple to munch.

Then came Sunday! I remember how we all loved to sing, my father especially. On early Sunday mornings he would play the organ in our front parlor, and we would all join in the hymn singing. In the hushed stillness of the quiet Sabbath morning, our voices would float out the open windows and could be heard all over the harbour. My father's two younger sisters, Aunts Lillian and Ethel, had beautiful voices, and both put this to good use in their long careers as wives of Salvation Army officers.

After Mom's Bible reading and Pop's prayers, we ate a hearty breakfast, maybe of cocoa and fisherman's brewis, then got dressed up in our Sunday best and all trooped off to the Barracks, leaving the dinner to cook at will. On Sunday mornings in winter, my father always had the porridge waiting as we dressed in front of the kitchen fire in our boys' long legged underwear, home-knit long black stockings and "golf socks." I know not why, as golf was an unknown quantity, but all the children wore home knit "golf socks" and that was that. As small children, we wore rubbers or spats over our high button-up shoes. As a teenager, I became the proud owner of my first pair of "Gaytees," an overshoe trimmed with fur.

We children attended Sunday morning service at 11:00 a.m., Sunday school at 2:00 p.m., and the evening service at 7:00 p.m. I'm afraid I don't remember much of those long-ago sermons, but I do remember one particular season and the lusty singing of a woman home from the States. She sat in a pew adjoining ours and wore much more fashionable clothes and hats than any of the local people. Instead of paying attention to the sermon, I longed for the time when I would be old enough and rich enough to wear such fine raiment and be the envy of all the other women in the church.

I was actually sometimes the envy of the other girls. My father's sister Lena lived in the States and her daughter, Lilith, was my age. What excitement when a box of her outgrown clothes would arrive on the steamer!

But usually we trotted off to church and school in homemade skirts or dresses always with a hand-knit sweater worn under our homemade coats. Some, like me, had clothes from family away, and others might be decked out from the Minister's barrel, humourously described by cousin Cyril in his first book years later.[3]

Slacks were unheard of. We felt not one whit deprived, as no one else owned a pair of slacks, either. Later, when we went tobogganing after school, or on a moonlit, frigid night, we draped ourselves in old pants or overalls of my father's.

We came home from morning service to a dinner of meat, often mutton, and vegetables, and always the same dessert on Sundays, jelly and blancmange. The mutton we had known in happier days as the sheep "Romeo" or "Oliver Twist" and if, at the time of sacrifice we gave them the passing tribute of a sigh, for we usually looked on them with a degree of affection, we nevertheless enjoyed the succulent roasts they provided.

One of my fond Sunday memories is of Uncle John Rowsell. He was father to Tom, and grandfather to Pierce, Walter, Ford, and the others. Uncle John was a very colourful character. He liked to be invited to different homes for dinner after Sunday

3 - *In Search of the Newfoundland Soul*, Harry Cuff Publications, 1982.

morning services. One Sunday, invited to our house, he partook of a meal with gusto, devouring huge amounts of mutton and vegetables. After he'd finished dessert, he leaned back with a satisfied sigh, and addressed my mother. "Ma'am, I hope I never drown, but if it's ever my lot to be drowned, I hope it's in a puncheon tub of this stuff," indicating the jelly and blancmange. However, Uncle John's end was not all that spectacular. They found him dead in bed, one morning, a peaceful smile on his wrinkled old face.

After the noon meal came Sunday school, in which my parents were involved. I remember my boldness in collecting for my Sunday school "Harvest Festival" Card, thereby making points with my Sunday school teacher. I would go from house to house collecting five- and ten-cent pieces. If I was turned down, it didn't faze me in the least. I would even board the *Clyde* and *Prospero* and approach the crew, from captain to deckhands, and I usually made a very good haul. In later years my boldness failed me, as I was easily intimidated by all and sundry and I never did realize the potential of my brash youth.

Class over, we were allowed a Sunday stroll. The commandment "Remember the Sabbath Day and keep it holy" was sternly obeyed in our home. No noisy games, no rowing, no picnics on the beach. If we were missing out we didn't know it, as all of our friends lived that way and we were perfectly happy.

Our favourite stroll on Sunday afternoons was to Spencer's Dock. En route we passed the graveyards, and spent many an hour reading the tombstones and smelling the wild roses blooming so profusely on the graves. We lingered at the graves of Grandma and Grandpa. They had a glistening white marble tombstone with their names, Edward and Lucy, and underneath, two hands entwined. Beneath the clasped hands was this verse:

There are thoughts that never perish
Bright, unfading through long years
So Thy memory we cherish
Shrined in hope, embalmed in tears.

I always left the graves saddened because my childish mind had never quite accepted the death of my beloved grandparents.

After a light "tea" maybe something left over, bread and molasses, and a tin of fruit, it was church time again. Even at a very young age, I enjoyed going to the Salvation Army Barracks, and I was especially enthralled by the various testimonies given by the converted souls sitting on the "platform." Their testimonies were repetitive, and we could repeat most of them verbatim.

The evening service was lively, the singing augmented by the beating of the big drum and the smaller kettledrum. After a sermon delivered with great passion and fervour, the prayer meeting ensued, at which time the sinners and backsliders were exhorted to come forward to the "penitent form." Carried away by the eloquence and the drama of it all, many nights the penitent form was filled with souls crying, confessing their sins, and then arising to testify to their conversion. Sad to say, their piety didn't always last. After some minor sin in the ensuing days, their tender consciences demanded that they declare themselves backsliders, and so the process began all over again. It was not thus with all the converts, many of whom remained true, year after year, and died, like my sainted grandmother, leaving behind beautiful memories of her faith.

The church's influence was strong. Cousin Cyril, at one time, aspired to be a preacher. On one occasion, on one of my holidays home from nursing, I heard him preach in the United Church. I was dumbfounded by his eloquence, his hidden talents being unknown to me. After all those years I still remember with what a flourish he ended his sermon: "In the words of John Oxenham."

To every man there cometh
A high way and a low
And the high soul seeks the high way
And the low soul gropes the low
While, in between, on the misty flats
The other run to and fro –
But to every man, there cometh

A high way and a low
And every man decideth
The way his soul must go –

It might well be that the world lost a second Billy Graham when Cyril left the ministry in favour of a brilliant career in the field of academics.

It Wasn't All Solemn

All holidays were looked forward to with much zest and anticipation, but Christmas was the big event of the year. The whole month of December was a glorious time. Our parents instilled in us the deeper meaning of Christmas, and we attended the pre-Christmas services with wonder and awe, but in our minds the Christmas concert held in the Orange Hall on Christmas Night was the highlight. For this we had practiced long hours after school, tramping home in the gloaming, past the lamplit houses, joyously pelting each other with snowballs, arriving home with ravenous appetites to consume endless slices of homemade bread with Avalon Creamery butter and partridgeberry jam, augmented by dried roast caplin, or boiled salt cod or baked beans with hot biscuits fresh out of the oven. This was supper, always served at 6:00 p.m., but our noon meal was dinner, mostly consisting of meat and vegetables. Then, too, there was a variation of pastries, soups, and stews. Occasionally someone would kill a sheep, and a mutton dinner was indeed a succulent feast.

But to get back to the concert. At last the big

night arrived, and off we went in white starched dresses, with pink sashes and pink hair bows. The Orange Lodge, which held a goodly number of people, was always filled to capacity. Proud mamas and papas and grandparents came to watch their children perform.

The concert was a hodgepodge of dialogues, monologues, recitations, songs, marches, and skits. Even the dignified Pierce Blackmore and Harold Warr entered into the spirit of the thing once, bringing down the house with their lively rendition of “Mr. Gallagher and Mr. Sheen.” At the concert’s close, Santa Claus came prancing in with his bells jingling merrily, and proceeded to give out the gifts that had been placed under the large, imposing tree. No one was forgotten. Our parents had brought the gifts earlier, putting them under the tree, or tying them to branches, and we fairly danced in frenzied suspense, waiting for our names to be called. The gifts were modest, but much more than our parents could really afford. How we gloated over our stockings, caps, and mittens, or storybooks, or the occasional doll. The extravaganza of toys now taken for granted was sadly lacking in those days.

After the exit of Santa, trays of homemade ice cream were passed around at the cost of five cents per cone. A rare treat indeed! We were content with one, knowing without being told that seconds were a complete impossibility.

A phase of Christmas, to which children and adults alike looked forward with great eagerness, was the mummering, or jannying, as we called it. From December 26 'till January 6, the nights were given over to jannying. We would disguise ourselves in the most impossible outfits, with crudely constructed false faces as grotesque as the individuals' ingenuity would allow, and sally forth from house to house banging on the doors and asking in a disguised voice, "Any jannies allowed in tonight?" Of course, everyone let us in, entering into the fun, trying to guess our identity.

The kitchens in which we were entertained were always so hot from the wood-burning stoves that as soon as we were identified, off would come our masks with a sigh of relief. Then would be produced the inevitable Christmas cake and a glass of syrup. The syrup was made from strawberry or raspberry concentrate, and nothing I've drunk before or since has tasted as good as that first reviving mouthful of syrup.

Some evenings we would stay home for the sheer pleasure of receiving jannies. Many of the grown-ups were mixed in with the young ones. We always had a lot of fun with Uncle Dorm. Uncle Dorm was a sober man who took life very seriously, but when he went jannying we saw a totally new side of him, which delighted us to no end. Perhaps his disguise gave him the courage to cavort in quite an unwonted style, but when he began his little dance, he was identified at once. He would dance around and sing his own special little ditty which I've never forgotten:

When you are going on a train
Never look out through the windowpane.
I did so once, to my regret
And won't do so again.
My pants were tight, and busted
And the passengers behind
Said "Oh, what a little short shirt you have
You'd better pull down the blind."

My father's moustache would twitch like mad, a sure sign of his merriment, and my mother would gaily cut the cake and pour the syrup. Later Christmases may have been more exotic and sophisticated, but none more thrilling than my childhood Christmases in Pilley's Island.

If Candlemas Day turned out to be gloomy and glum, we eagerly awaited Easter as a harbinger of spring. On Good Friday, the family tradition was to fast until noon. Then in the afternoon the men went trout fishing while the womenfolk stayed home to get things in readiness for Easter Sunday, with extra baking, cleaning, and attention to detail. There were always church services on the evening of Good Friday.

On Easter Sunday we all went to 7:00 a.m. knee drill, which meant we stayed on our knees during the entire service, then back home for breakfast of porridge and boiled eggs, the latter having been painstakingly collected from our six laying hens which didn't always produce as they should. Furthermore, in their wandering about, the hens made their nests in the most unusual places: the barn, the cookhouse, the different sheds or the sawdust pit. We were hard put to find them, so that a meal of unlimited eggs was a luxury indeed.

On Sunday afternoon there was an Easter cantata put on by the Sunday school, for which we spent hours of practice. Then the evening service at night rounded off our day. So, on Easter Sunday, we had our fill of prayer and praise. The next day we begged our mother to let us discard our long-legged underwear. If she finally relented, we felt we had gained a major victory.

After Easter, the next celebration was Mother's Day. On that day, each person wore a rose: red if the mother was living, white if she was deceased. On that day, too, a concert was held with singing and recitations on the subject of mothers, and we made a concerted effort to help all we could, and be model children. Needless to say, the next day saw us back to our normal impish selves.

Another red-letter day on our island, enjoyed by young and old alike, was the Sunday school picnic. Somehow it never rained on those occasions. I remember waking to cloudless skies, the sun dancing merrily on the harbour and with a wild sense of anticipation. The picnic was always held in Anthony's long sloping meadow, our "village green." The previous day was spent in preparing food, which was placed on long trestle tables, and enjoyed while someone played a fiddle in the background. Then the games started: tug-of-war, sack race, one-legged race, and a lot of old English and Scottish games brought from the old country. I think what I liked best were the "Rings." We would hold hands, form a huge circle, then sing "The Grand Old Duke of York," and "The Farmer in the Dell." From the choosing of one of the boys to be the farmer, to the wife, the child, the nurse, the dog, the bone, and then reversing it as the farmer leaves his wife, etc. until at the end, we sang:

The bone stands alone
The bone stands alone
Hi ho the deary oh
The bone stands alone.

Then we repeated the procedure. It was a thrill to be part of that magic circle. Although compared with today's entertainment it must sound incredibly rustic and dull, those happy, carefree days of long-ago picnics were a wonderful, integral part of my childhood.

Feeding the Mind

School attendance was not compulsory in those days. Many of the children dropped out of school, the boys to work in the lumber woods or the cod fisheries on the French Shore and Labrador, the girls to work as housemaids, or to marry and settle down to raising a family.

True, the tuition was modest compared with today's monetary standards, but my parents, though sometimes hard-pressed to meet the monthly school bills, vowed that somehow each child would get an education, and, at no small sacrifice, that was accomplished. Aunt Blanche and Uncle Dorm were equally adamant in their determination to educate their children.

Instead of grades we took Primary, Preliminary, Intermediate, and Junior Associate. This was the extent of our education in Pilley's Island. Our subjects included English, French, Mathematics (arithmetic, trigonometry, and algebra), English History, and Physiography.

In our early years, we attended the one-room Salvation Army School. It was pleasant in spring and early fall, walking to school, but the winter months were difficult. It was about a ten minute walk if we took the shortcut around shore. We sometimes plowed through waist-high snowdrifts, with school bag in one hand, and a junk of wood under the other arm. To keep the pot-bellied stove in the centre of the room going, it was a strict requirement that each child bring his or her daily quota of one piece of firewood.

Being Britain's oldest colony, our education was British-oriented. In early years we studied English pounds, shillings, and pence, and weights and measures. However, we never used English money. At that time Newfoundland had its own currency.

We were well-versed in British history, tracing the royal lineage to its early beginnings. We memorized dates of battles, a few of them being the Battle of Trafalgar, the Wars of the Roses, the Seven Years War, the battles of Flodden and Sheriffmuir, and so on. Every night we had to study a chapter of English history, and be ready to answer any questions about it the next day. Any child derelict in his or her homework would get a stiff caning. I can still see cousin Una standing in front of the teacher's desk, taking four strokes on either hand, sobbing pitifully. I made sure my homework was always finished, as I wasn't anxious to bear either the pain or the humiliation of the teacher's strap.

Our school work was done with slate and pencil, and our homework with scribblers and lead pencil. Our copy books were done in pen and ink.

No such thing as Bic in those days, just a pen with a nib that had to be dipped frequently in the inkwell or ink bottle. Those pens were the bane of my existence.

We also had a geography book and a book of hygiene. But the focal point of our studies was the "Royal Reader." At the end of Grade I we proceeded to the Royal Reader of Grade II, and so on through Grade VI. The Royal Reader covered a lot of territory. It was an education in itself. Any attempt of mine to describe the Royal Readers would pale in comparison to the graphic description written by cousin Cyril's *In Search of the Newfoundland Soul*. Enough to say that the Royal Readers covered a wide spectrum of useful knowledge, and created in me an insatiable thirst for learning, and a love of prose and poetry that has enhanced my life.

Every spare moment we Poole girls could steal, we read. Through Aunt Susie Vineham and her books from the hospital library I had my first introduction to Charles Dickens, William Thackeray, and Victor Hugo, and such volumes of poets as Shakespeare, Keats, Byron, and Shelley. My mother, Gladys, and Geneva shared in the spoils. We would memorize poems that have stayed with me to this day. Of course, the classics and poetry couldn't fill the void inside of us that clamoured for romance, and in addition to those in Aunt Susie's bookcase we collected most of the works of Ethel

M. Dell, Mary J. Holmes, Mrs. E. P. Roe, and Margaret Pedlar. In our early years we had been introduced to the Elsie Dinsmore books that my mother had managed to collect. How we wept and rejoiced with Elsie in her defeats and her victories. My mother held her up to us as a paragon of virtue – she was really too good to be true, and how far we strayed from following in her footsteps!

In summer, we usually went to bed before lamplighting time. If we wanted to finish a book we were reading, we would go outside on the porch steps to catch the last glimmer of daylight until Mom summoned us in for bed, cautioning us against "straining our eyes."

On stormy days we took our lunch and spent lunchtime around the school stove with a sandwich of moose meat, or beans, and drinking cold tea from a Nujol[4] bottle.

It was all great fun, and we thoroughly enjoyed lunchtime. It was a matter of pride that, no matter how hard times were, we were never reduced to having to bring lobster to school for lunch. Only the very poorest would eat lobster, a preference later discovered to be not unique to Pilley's Island.

Recess time, from eleven to eleven-thirty, was keenly anticipated. We would troop out to the back shed-like porch, unmindful of the freezing temperatures, and there play games like blind man's bluff,

4 - a type of mineral oil

pin the tail on the donkey, and post office, until the school bell rang, and we reluctantly went back to our long, iron-legged wooden desks that seated three on either side. The outhouse was situated on a grassy knoll overlooking a steep bank. Once, during a bad storm, the structure blew over. Fortunately no one was in it at the time.

An event that comes back in my memory where it has lain dormant for seventy years concerns Winnie Poole, who was a bit older than I. The older girls sometimes were called upon to pray at the end of the Bible verses session. This day the teacher said, "At the end of the Bible verses, Winnie Poole will pray." I was about six and I thought I heard the teacher say, "Gwennie Poole will pray," so I had little time to improvise. When the time came for the prayer, I started in with great assurance and volubility but was promptly made to end my exhortation and commanded in no uncertain terms to "sit down." Bitter humiliation, but not the last. One morning Bible verse would begin with the letter "A," the next morning "B," and so on. We would go through the alphabet frequently. One day I forgot a verse beginning with "A," so I quickly improvised, "And the Lord spoke unto Moses, saying," for which I was quickly censured by the teacher, who informed me that that was an incomplete verse, and once again I bowed my head in overwhelming shame. It was quite a disgrace to forget your verse. One day Doug Ward couldn't remember his verse beginning with "G." In desperation, he looked down at his desk and blurted, "God bless this little desk."

Dougie Ward was usually called by the nickname "Scuse." One morning when he was late for school, he gave the teacher some trumped-up reason for his tardiness. The teacher said, "That's no excuse, Douglas," and he came back with "Bad 'scuse better'n narn." Scuse and Max Blackmore were buddies, and their escapades drove the teacher crazy, and kept us all on edge, wondering what was coming next! Doug was not a vindictive boy, but he followed Max's bullying orders without question. It was a relief when Max's family moved to Bell Island, where his father had gotten a job working in the mines.

Most of the school kids had a nickname, and sometimes the names changed. Except for one winter, when making angels in the snow while wearing a coat with fancy braiding on the back earned her the nickname Monument, Geneva was called Prospero. I must explain that the SS *Prospero* was larger than the *Clyde*, making trips from St. John's all the way to points north as far as St. Anthony. It was a longer trip, and more involved. It was a thrilling sight to see the *Prospero* looming in the narrows which were barely wide enough to accommodate her. To our childish vision she was truly a formidable sight, hence Geneva's nickname.

Of us all, Gladys was the intellectual giant. She could read and write at the age of four and surprised everyone with the amount of knowledge stored in that small head. As she grew, she became more introspective and quiet. She was a voracious reader, and sometimes, seemingly, she inhabited another planet. She had no athletic ability or mechanical skills whatsoever. She did household chores with an air of detachment, as if her mind were elsewhere, as indeed it was. Perhaps because she stayed aloof from shenanigans, Gladys was called "Purity." One day, walking home from school, daydreaming no doubt, with a slight smile on her face, she was accosted by some of the rough boys with "What are you smiling for?" Gladys replied, "I suppose it's anyone's privilege to smile whenever they want." Privilege was to us a big word, and from then on Gladys was called "Privilege."

The September that Gladys was ready for Intermediate, the teacher at the Salvation Army School didn't have that grade herself, and so my mother enrolled her in the United Church School. The highly indignant teacher summoned my mother to the school and said, "If I'm not capable of teaching Gladys, then perhaps I'm not capable of teaching Geneva either," to which my mother promptly agreed, and we were all transferred to the UC school. I think I was in Grade six. My mother felt that the teaching in the United Church School was superior, as indeed it was, and she was determined to give us the best education available on the Island.

Annual Highlights

New Year's Eve meant little or nothing to us as children. It came and went unmarked by fuss and fanfare, but even though I was only five, I vividly remember the New Year's Eve that ushered in the year of 1920. As my mother, pregnant with Madge, born July 31 of that year, hung up the pretty new calendar for 1920 from Gerald S. Doyle, beside our eight-day clock, she remarked to my father how times were changing and becoming modernized. My father, in one of his wild flights of fancy, predicted all sorts of futuristic events in the decade so newly born. My mother laughed and said "Jess, your imagination is running away with you," but he just shook his head, his moustache twitching, and replied, "Just wait, Millie, just you wait and see." His predictions about aeronautics and transportation and communications have long since been realized, though not in the 1920s.

As we became teenagers we celebrated the New Year by attending house parties, usually at Melene Whalen's or Margaret Blackmore's. We played games like Charades, Musical Chairs, Animal, Mineral, or Vegetable Kingdom, and sometimes card games like Rook, Flinch, and Forty-fives. When we got home, regardless of the time, Mom would be sitting in her rocking chair by the kitchen fire, her knitting, as always, in her lap, and eagerly waiting to hear all about the party. Sometimes we would celebrate with a Box party, at the schoolhouse. We girls would draw a number for partners at games and, later, to walk us home. It was all thoroughly relived again that night and well into the next day.

We looked forward to Candlemas, February 2. In the U.S. it's known as Groundhog Day, but there being no groundhogs in Newfoundland, we called it by the English Church name of Candlemas Day. From my mother we learned the ditty:

If Candlemas Day be fair and fine
The worst of the winter is left behind
If Candlemas Day be gloomy and glum
The worst of the winter is yet to come.

We took this forecast quite literally, and rejoiced to see a sunshiny day, firmly convinced that winter storms and huge snowbanks would soon be a thing of the past. But if the day was gloomy, we braced ourselves for yet more slogging through the snow-drifts, and an extension of wearing boys' long-legged underwear.

On Valentine's Day, it was the custom to kiss your favourite people in the hope of a gift in return.

My father once was kissed by Margaret Blackmore, and he gave her a cup and saucer, much to my mother's dismay. Being quite fearless in those days of my callow youth, one year I decided to kiss all three leading merchants. I arrived home from this adventure carrying a box of stationery from Harold Warr, a box of handkerchiefs from Pierce Blackmore, and last but not least, a cake of Palmolive soap from Mike Whalen. Kissing the last took a great deal of courage, but I figured the cake of Palmolive soap was well worth the effort. Gladys and Geneva applauded my temerity, but stopped short of following my example, Gladys because she was too shy and proud, Geneva because she was too proud.

May 24 was the best single holiday of the year for us. Being Empire Day, the schools were closed, and so the young set crowded into Roland Ginn's motorboat and set off to Little Bay Islands, about two hours-motor away – for a day of fun. The people of Little Bay Islands were a very hospitable lot. At noon there was picnic food in abundance, followed by games and races, winding up with the big event of the day, a football game between Little Bay Islands and Little Bay. We liked to root for the Little Bay boys, especially the Wells brothers, George and Charlie, the latter of whom became Geneva's husband. After the game and supper, we proceeded to the Orange Lodge for the play that rounded out the evening. The play would be humorous, well-planned and well-acted, although, of course, rank amateur. About midnight we would set off for the return trip home, arriving in the early morning hours, tired and content.

One year we didn't make it home. The weather turned cold and very windy and we had to depend on the good souls of Little Bay Islands to house us for the night. Geneva, Una, and I were put up at the parsonage. The lovely minister's wife was most hospitable and kind. The thing I remember most is how we three got in bed together and shivered with cold all night. Too bashful to ask for extra blankets, we piled our coats on the bed, to no avail. An icy wind, blowing off the icebergs in the harbour, seemed to penetrate the very walls. Relieved when morning came, after having had very little sleep, we thankfully boarded the motorboat for our return home. The sun was shining, the bay was calm, and, as we usually did on such excursions, we sang all the way home. Our bone-chilling experience of the previous night was soon forgotten, and in no way spoiled the memory of an otherwise glorious day.

We always had a fancy costume party at Halloween, held in the schoolhouse. The games were hilarious, and there was always a prize for the most original costume. I remember one such Halloween. Geneva laboured hard and long over costumes for the both of us, Madge being still too young. She fashioned a Japanese kimono for me out of the numerous pieces of material our mother kept in an old trunk. Then she tied my hair in a pigtail, put cocoa paper on my cheeks (there being a lack of rouge), and a bit of stove blacking to emphasize my eyebrows. I practiced mincing steps and felt like a true geisha girl. As for her, she went as "Night" in a long black satin gown, made from the same old trunk treasures. On the back she sewed a magnificent silver moon, and silver stars dotted the front and sleeves. I was certain she would take the prize. Much to our chagrin and dismay, Winnie Rideout, in a nurse's uniform, was pronounced the most original! We both agreed that the judges didn't know the meaning of the word, and that they suffered from a lack of imagination, and couldn't recognize talent when it was staring them in the face. However, that didn't dampen our enthusiasm, and we both had a great time, finally escorted home by a couple of boys from Little Bay Islands.

On November 5 we carried out the old English tradition of Guy Fawkes Day, or Bonfire Night in Newfoundland terms. Guy Fawkes Day is the anniversary of the Gunpowder Plot (1605) to blow up the King and the Houses of Parliament. At night, huge bonfires were lit to burn grotesque stuffed figures called "Guys." That was how it had been celebrated in England, but in Newfoundland the tradition was still being carried on, burning huge boughs and Christmas trees. Our Island was plentifully loaded with trees of all kinds, and ours for the taking. We would tramp in the woods days before the big night, and gather large stacks of boughs. As we were ten children in both families, there was no shortage of help. The younger ones went along, not so much to help as to enjoy the fun. Dragging out the boughs was not a chore – we looked forward to it, Roy being the leader.

Every family on the Island was equally determined to accumulate as many boughs as possible, the object being to see who could keep the bonfire going the longest. Usually the Poole clan was named the winner.

House parties were big on our agenda. Insular as we were, closely knit and familiar with people's birthdays, we used them as an excuse for a party. Led by Elsie Boyd, who worked in Pierce Blackmore's store and lived with the Blackmores, and Margaret Blackmore, and armed with food, we would descend on the unsuspecting birthday boy or girl, or even on one of the elders, and have a riotous time playing parlour games far into the night. However, none of these fun things could take place until our evening chores were complete: the woodbox filled, the water barrel filled and the flour for the night's breadmaking brought from a huge barrel of flour stored in a small outside shed, also the repository of barrels of pork, beef, and a keg of molasses.

Our own birthdays passed with little fanfare.

No gaily wrapped gifts or elaborate cakes, but the first week in August we would celebrate our combined birthdays, Madge's (July 31), mine (August 2), and Gladys's (August 13) by having a picnic out on "the rocks," a portion of land jutting out from Valentine Manuel's (a small cove across the harbour from our house always known to us simply as Valentine Manuel's, although I have no idea who he was). The birthdays of our other family members, Mom's and Pop's in January, Don's in March, and Geneva's in October, slipped by with little to mark the passing of the years.

When I was fourteen, I had a huge crush on Claude Payne. He was twenty-eight and my mother soon squelched the romance, but I would sometimes sneak away and go for a walk with Claude to Spencer's Dock. Claude had a large, closed-in motorboat and, that fall, he took six of us to Triton to a barn dance. My mother, thinking there was safety in numbers, reluctantly allowed me to go along, especially as cousin Una was in the party. At that time she was dating Hayward Giles. Also, the Salvation Army schoolteacher, Cecil Pretty, went along. At the time he was dating Elsie Boyd, who was much older than Una and me. It was a gorgeous, moonlit night and we were singing as we sped down the tickle when, suddenly, the motor just died, and there we were, marooned until the next morning, when a fisherman spied us and towed us back to Pilley's. Although we were all together throughout the night, I felt that somehow I had been compromised and was most subdued and penitent. After that I didn't see much of Claude, except for the times we skated together on the harbour, which was frozen from December to March. Claude was a terrific skater and I loved crossing hands with him and skating in the moonlight.

How can I describe the moonlight expeditions of the winter months? With our breath forming moisture on the woolen scarves around our necks and our hands encased in two pairs of mittens, we piled on the catamaran and coasted down steep hills with one of the boys as driver. Then we would plod back up the hill to repeat the experience. When the harbour froze over and became a glassy sheet of ice, we went skating in the moonlight with a bunch of boys and girls. I would be enchanted if the aforementioned Claude Payne appeared on the scene, smelling of delicious aftershave, and picked me for his partner. We would link hands and traverse the harbour and I would be in seventh heaven. Geneva, supposedly seeking to protect her little sister, set her cap for Claude and, very soon, I was abandoned in favour of Geneva's charms. I really didn't mind as Geneva was my idol and could do no wrong. With the fickleness of youth, I soon transferred my affections to a boy somewhat nearer my age.

Surviving

After the mine closed down and the small mine hospital disbanded, Margaret Blackmore became community nurse. Once, my mother sought her advice when she was desperately worried about Geneva, who had developed erysipelas in her right arm, an acute infectious disease of the skin. Today, thanks to the wonder of drugs, the term and the condition are virtually unknown, but then it was quite a prevalent and serious disease. Margaret took one look at Geneva's swollen, infected arm and, with her superior air and Twillingate twang, she declared, "The child must be taken to Twillingate Hospital to have her arm amputated." My mother, rightly or wrongly, stated she would rather see Geneva dead than go through life minus her right arm. In any event, she was determined that neither would happen, and with the help of her trusty "doctor's book," she cured Geneva's arm and my sister's right arm remained intact and functioning.

Actually, the death rate on the Island in those days was amazingly low, in view of the fact that there was no medical aid available and certain diseases were rampant. Occasionally someone fell ill with what was termed "inflammation of the bowels," and a speedy death ensued. With my later acquired medical knowledge, I suspected that this was doubtless due to a ruptured appendix, but there was no one to make a true diagnosis.

I often thought back to those experiences after I'd started my nurse's training. One such occasion stands out in my memory. While I was visiting Head's Harbour with Aunt Blanche, her brother Horace was suddenly taken with an attack of renal colic. Watching him writhing in agony on the kitchen couch, we were all sympathetic but helpless. After a great deal of pain, he finally passed the kidney stone, thereby gaining quick relief.

In later years, when I had my first attack of renal colic at the Nurses' Home of the TB Sanitarium in St. John's where I was on the staff, I was afforded immediate relief by a quarter grain of morphine, administered by the resident physician, Dr. Knowling. I thought back to Head's Harbour and Horace Watkins and what the poor man must have suffered prior to getting rid of that stone.

Tuberculosis was the main scourge of so many of the small outports of Newfoundland, and ours was no exception. How our two families survived with no casualties was a miracle. On our way to the mines one day to pick blueberries, Aunt Blanche and I stopped at the Fifields' for a glass of water. The Fifields had several daughters, mostly teenagers, and there on a couch by the window lay a girl of about fifteen in the last states of tuberculosis, with feverish cheeks, glassy eyes, and a racking cough. It was evident, even to my untutored eyes, that she wasn't long for this world. Aunt Blanche cut our visit short, but we did get our glass of water and left, rather saddened and subdued. Bessie Fifield died the following week, and most of her family followed in quick succession.

My mother, with no medical help she trusted when emergencies arose, fell back entirely on her own ingenuity and her precious "doctor's book." Where she got it, I don't know, but it was there from my earliest remembrance. It was a huge book, so heavy I couldn't lift it when I was small. It covered every childhood disease, as well as the ills of older people and, without it, our household could hardly have functioned. Young Gladys, being of an inquiring mind, would sneak to the big trunk at the top of the stairs, drag out the book, and pour over the graphic pictures. Once, being caught and reprimanded by our mother, she looked up with her winsome smile and said, "Mommy, all I read was 'wrap him in warm blankets.'"

We had the usual run of childhood diseases. With no inoculations, we ran the gamut of whooping cough, chicken pox, measles, and a mysterious ailment that we were all subjected to from time to time: nausea, vomiting, and diarrhea that lasted for two or three days. Mom called it a "bilious attack" but, since then, I have decided it was nothing more or less than food poisoning. We had no refrigeration, of course, and I'm sure that tainted food was the culprit.

In spite of it all, we were surprisingly healthy, which we could attribute, no doubt, to the outdoor living and daily exercise of climbing hills and rowing boats. Our island air was so clean and unpolluted that if we put a table out on the verandah and let it stay there for days, it never gathered dust or grime. My father and Uncle Dorm were hardy fishermen and hunters and, no doubt, the exposure to fresh air and exercise in winter and summer kept them in excellent shape.

Also, our diet boasted no junk foods, little candy and no pop. There was always fresh garden produce and plenty of seafood: codfish, cod tongues, trout, salmon, herring, and lobster, as well as caplin and mussels, which we all loved. Then, in the summer, we had an ample supply of wild strawberries, raspberries, blueberries, partridgeberries, squashberries, and bakeapples. All were bottled in huge quantities to last us through the winter months. Our goats and a few laying hens provided us with milk and eggs. Moose and caribou meat was abundant all winter, also geese, partridge, and turrs. Rabbit, of course, was our staple meat all winter, a favourite meal being rabbit soup. Coming home from school on a late, frosty winter afternoon, it was comforting to find a big pot of rabbit soup on the stove, complete with rice, carrots, turnips, parsnips, and potatoes, topped off with dumplings.

Also, if peas and beans be good diet, then we were surely blessed: pea soup every Saturday, and baked beans with homemade rolls twice a week. A great favourite was the boiled dinner, salt beef with cabbage, potatoes, turnips, and carrots, and sometimes, if we were lucky, pease pudding and dumplings or boiled bread pudding. The word cholesterol was not in our lexicon and we survived the sodium and fat from salt beef and pork. My father lived to be ninety-five and my mother ninety-three.

My mother was always well-stocked with old-fashioned remedies than ran the gamut of all-out childhood illnesses and accidents, as well as the more sophisticated potions and pills for the adults. There was Dr. Chase's Nerve Food Pills that I already mentioned as possibly helping my mother through her nervous breakdown. Then there were Dodd's Kidney Pills, which my father took frequently for the backaches that were a natural aftermath of the heavy loads of game and logs that he carried on his shoulders and the other back strains incidental to his work. Also, Dodd's Little Liver Pills seemed to give him great comfort. Then there were Radways Ready Relief for his stomach woes, Nujol Oil for the bowels, Sloan's Liniment, Minard's Liniment, and Eclectic Oil for massage.

We had camphorated oil for chest rubs, linseed meal poultices, hot onion poultices, and hot bread poultices for boils and suppurating sores. Every spring we got doses of sulphur and molasses to cleanse our systems and act as a tonic after the long winter months. Our biggest bugaboo was the dreaded "senna tea" whenever we got what my mother called "the bilious attack." On would go the kettle, and soon the aroma of senna tea would fill the house. If, as was usually the case, we were confined to bed, my mother would bring the senna to our bedside and watch over us with an eagle eye until we drank it. How we longed to dump it into the chamber pot, but we suffered. With the resiliency of youth, we quickly recovered, and none the worse for the experience. There was also a tonic called Beef, Iron and Wine that people felt was a cure for the winter blahs. Sometimes my father would return from the stores to report sadly that the shelves were empty of this magic potion, and we all knew why. Lacking the real thing, it was the only substitute the few imbibers on the island had for some of their drunken sprees.

I might add that neither my father nor mother ever tasted alcoholic beverages, not even a beer. On one summer holiday, when Don and I happened to be home together, he brought a bottle of rum and we went up to Lorabatt's Pond and had a glorious time, swimming, drinking, and sunbathing, after which we rowed home, slightly drunk and in great humour. Mom and Pop had no idea of the cause of our high spirits, and Mom remarked to Pop that she was pleased to see Gwen and Don so happy and enjoying their holiday.

My father had one serious illness that may have killed a weaker man. He had a disorder of the middle ear that caused infection to spread to the mastoid. Due to antibiotics, the term "mastoiditis" is seldom heard today but, when my dad fell ill in the early '30s, he rapidly worsened with high fever, excruciating pain, and a stiff neck. My sister Gladys, who was in training at the Grace Hospital in St. John's at the time, did a terrific job in getting our father transported to St. John's by way of the SS *Prospero*, which made weekly trips from St. John's to the far north. How my father survived the three-day trip en route in less than ideal surroundings is a miracle. At the Grace they immediately did a mastoidectomy, but he developed general septicemia and the prospects looked dire.

One day my mother received a telegram saying "Temperature 106, expect the worst." When I saw her ironing a white sheet with painstaking care, the tears streaming down her face, I realized for what purpose the sheet was intended: a shroud for my father! However, he slowly recovered enough that he could be sent home again by steamer, accompanied by Gladys. Nursing him back to health was a job that involved us all – we would take turns at night watches. It was a long, long time before he could again resume his strenuous life.

Our financial resources were nil, and it was a

tough blow to my mother's pride when we had to go on the "dole" that winter for the very first time, and last time, even during the Great Depression. I was fourteen and a half and Geneva almost eighteen, and we were both determined to find work. The only thing available was housework. Geneva took work as a live-in housemaid for the family of the Salvation Army Officer stationed in Pilley's Island.

I took a housemaid's job in Head's Harbour with Wesley and Netta Pittman. They had four children and it was no easy task. I received board and room and the grand sum of seven dollars per month, quite a fortune in those days.

Head's Harbour was about forty-five minutes away, accessible only by boat in summer and dog team or hiking on the ice in winter, and I didn't get home very often. But, one weekend, a young man named Ralph Watkins, a nephew of Aunt Blanche, and I walked on the ice to Bumble Bee Bight, then on up the harbour until we finally reached my home. We set out to return in early evening the next day. The sky looked threatening and my mother predicted a snowstorm, but we thought we'd make it back ahead of the storm. Instead, like in the story of Lucy Gray in one of our readers, the storm came on before its time. It was a scary experience. Ralph made me push my face deep in my big woollen scarf and close my eyes, and he led me through the blizzard of no small proportions. We wandered for many hours before we saw the lamplit windows of Head's Harbour. The news of our safe arrival didn't reach my mother until three days later. I've always been grateful to Ralph and, years later in my senior year of nursing, I was saddened to hear of his untimely death by drowning when his dog team and sled went through the ice in Raft Tickle.

The accidents and misadventures of our childhood were too numerous to mention, but a few stick out in my mind. When Gladys was about ten, she fell in the hold of a schooner on a pile of ballast rocks and split her skull open. Not skilful at suturing, my mother did the best she could and Gladys recovered. She probably sustained a skull fracture, but who was to know – Mom's stitches, nature, and the Good Lord took care of the healing.

The many times we fell overboard over the wharf head are legion. It's a paradox that, growing up on the Atlantic Ocean with beaches all around, so few of us learned to swim. The younger boys could swim like fish, but Roy, Una, Gladys, Geneva, and I never did learn. Gladys could float on her back a little and Madge could dog-paddle, but I never did learn anything, in spite of Ford Rowsell's valiant efforts to teach me.

Once Roy barely survived his dunking. We were all fishing for tomcods off the wharf head when Roy took a tumble in the deep water. We all ran for help and met my grandfather, who couldn't make sense of his excited grandchildren, all talking together. Fortunately, my mother, who had been gathering eggs in the nearby barn, grasped the situation immediately. There was a big skiff moored off the wharf and, with superhuman strength, my mother caught the painter and pulled it in just far enough to clamber into it. Roy was going down for the third and probably last time when she clutched his fingers and managed to hold his head above water until Grandpa could pull the chubby boy into the boat.

As for me, I seemed to be more accident-prone than most. One bonfire night, November 5, we were all cavorting around our bonfire and yelling like banshees when Max Blackmore threw a lighted bough into the air which fell on me, igniting my clothing. Doug Ward, with great presence of mind, rolled me in his overcoat, extinguishing the flames, but not before I was badly burned on my neck. My mother applied eclectic oil and put me to bed, where I lay sleepless and suffering all night long. To this day, I carry the scar on my neck, mute testimony to that long-ago accident. It was rather an anticlimax to an otherwise wild old celebration – I was kept home from school a few days, and treated to some rare pampering by the whole family.

Perhaps my most painful accident happened when I was about twelve. On a beautiful August morning, Geneva and I decided to spend the day on Valentine Manuel's slopes picking raspberries. It was our favourite spot, hilly and densely wooded, with the large raspberries hanging down like grapes in the open areas. Happily, without a care in the world, we rowed across the harbour to the opposite shore, about ten minutes away. We beached our row-boat and began the climb. The sun was shining, the birds were singing, the harbour peaceful, save for the putt-putt of the occasional motorboat. We picked to our heart's content, filling our gallon cans in record time, chattering gaily all the while. Suddenly, I stepped directly into a hornets' nest and was immediately surrounded by a cloud of them. I screamed for "Neve," who yelled, "Run for the water."

We had always been told about this very real threat and that, should it happen, the water was the best place to run to, as the hornets would then disappear. I ran, slipping and sliding down the hill, still carefully holding my berries. By the time I reached the beach and waded in, I couldn't see – the stings covered my arms, face, and neck – my eyes were swollen shut, and I was a pitiful-looking mess, sobbing with pain. Geneva, right behind me with her pail of berries also still intact, rowed home as fast as she could. My mother, for once, didn't stop to consult her doctor's book. She hustled me in around shore to the home of Stanley Simmons, who was then living in Uncle Billy Witt's house. Stanley was a World War I veteran and had brought back as his bride an English nurse. She applied some sort of soothing poultices and gave me aspirin, the strongest painkiller available. I still recall the misery of that night, and it was days before my face returned to normal.

Nothing daunted, our berry picking was soon resumed: raspberries on Valentine Manuel's, blueberries on the mines and on Hackett's Island, a small rocky prominence in the middle of the harbour literally covered with blueberries. Earlier, there would be wild strawberries in profusion, and our favourite haunt for them was Tom Tilley's path, on the other side of Lorabatt's Cove. On one occasion we wandered far afield, lured by the enticing strawberries, until suddenly we realized we were lost. Gladys, the impractical dreamer, rose beautifully to the occasion, climbing a tall tree to find our whereabouts, and discovering the church spire in the distance, she safely shepherded us home.

Years after I left the island, my mother once again sought Margaret Blackmore's advice, as a last resort. My brother, Don, then fifteen, was very ill with pneumonia. By that time antibiotics were on the market and Margaret prescribed sulfanilamide, which was all to the good, but she continued to give it after he improved. My mother, alarmed by his blueness and general malaise, wired me in St. John's. I had finished training and was working with the American Forces in their Engineer Hospital at Fort Pepperell in St. John's. I sought and obtained a week's leave and went home, taking Madge, who was in her last year of nurse's training at the Grace, with me.

When we arrived, we were alarmed to find Don with blue lips, glassy eyes, and gasping for breath. I immediately stopped the medication and poured fluids into him. In a couple of days, we saw marked improvement and, from then on, he continued to improve so that Madge and I could return to our respective hospitals with feelings of thankfulness and relief.

As hardy as he was, there was no help for Uncle Dorm in the fall of 1946 when he contracted tularemia. Tularemia is an acute bacterial disease also known as rabbit fever because it is sometimes transmitted to humans from rabbits, as it was to Uncle Dorm through a cut in his hand.[5]

It was a terrible irony given how rabbits had always been such a staple in our lives. My father never really recovered from Dorm's death and, being over sixty at the time, lost all heart for the work he and his brother had always done together.

5 - With symptoms of fever and chills, Dorm was taken by boat to Twillingate hospital, accompanied by sixteen-year-old Joyce. The experienced Dr. Olds was away and, with the antidote for tularemia readily available, a younger doctor misdiagnosed his condition and treated him for pneumonia. A few years later that same doctor, lecturing to a nursing class which included Joyce, informed the class that the only known death in Newfoundland from tularemia was Miss Poole's father.

Leaving the Nest

Both families being adherents of the Salvation Army, it was only natural that sisters Gladys and later Geneva attended the S.A. Teachers Training College, and spent some years in teaching. Gladys was a sweet, loving sister to me, and when she left home at the age of sixteen, I missed her terribly and keenly anticipated her holidays when she would return for two weeks, bringing Margaret Pedlar books and stories of her adventures in the great outside world.

With Gladys's absence, Madge being only six and Don a baby, Geneva and I became inseparable. I admired and envied her competence and skill. She could do all the things I longed to do but was so very inept in the doing. She sewed beautifully. She could knit, do fancy work, cook and bake, and on one occasion, she even constructed a piano for our playhouse. It was made from a large wooden biscuit box, with a keyboard complete with black and white keys. In addition to her practical side, she was also a bookworm and dreamer, and through her flights of imagination, Geneva and I were often transported into a different world.

On a long, lazy summer afternoon, Geneva and I would take a blanket and book, climb the hill above our house, and there, in a field of sweet-smelling clover, we would lie and dream. To this day, when I see and smell clover, I can close my eyes and visualize two young girls, so incredibly naive and untried, with the skies a delicate blue above the deeper blue of the peaceful harbour, the silence of the distant hills, the drone of the bees, and the putt-putt of a far-off motor. Recalling my childhood, one of my sharpest memories is a field of clover and impossible dreams.

We often dreamed and talked about the day we would leave our island, go out into the big, wide world, and carve a niche for ourselves. I loved our primitive existence, but Geneva could hardly wait for that day and she too left home at sixteen to enter the Teachers Training College.

I missed Geneva terribly, but by this time Madge was growing up, and we became very close. Madge, too, was a bookworm, and we shared books and poetry, confidences and dreams. It was a quiet time, unmarked by the turbulence of growing up with Gladys and Geneva. Madge was easy to live with, except for the time I snitched her best pair of nylons and got a run in them. She didn't speak to me for two whole days. I tried to placate her with a cup and saucer, but that didn't work either. But Madge being Madge, it was against her nature to hold a grudge, so we finally made up, and I don't think we've had a falling-out since.

We would write our final exams the third week in June. Then the papers would be sent to St. John's for grading, and it would be the middle of August before we got the results. It never really spoiled our summers, as we were all pretty sure of ourselves. Two teachers of that time come to mind, Robert Horwood and Philip Forsey of the United Church School, both dedicated, highly intelligent young men, outstanding in their field.

Philip Forsey was from Grand Bank, quite a handsome, intelligent young man, and, of course, we all had schoolgirl crushes on him. I was a plain Jane and couldn't hope to compete with the prettier girls, Winnie Rideout, Gertie Tizzard, and Doris Cobb. But, sometimes after reading an essay or composition of mine, he would sit at my desk and discuss it and then suggest different poets and authors that he thought I might like. I was grateful for those small crumbs of interest, and after he, one day, in a rare mood of confidence, predicted I would go far, I was on cloud nine for days.

Phil boarded with Auntie "Blink" Budgell, and that Christmas she confided in me that he had purchased two boxes of chocolates, one larger than the other. He told her he couldn't decide who was to get the larger one, me or Doris Cobb, whose fluffy good looks had him somewhat mesmerized. I remember I was surprised and delighted at the unexpected gift – and Auntie later told me it was the larger box. Score one for me!

While awaiting the results of Junior Associate, or Junior Matriculation, as it later became known, I received a telegram from my teacher, Philip Forsey, who was spending the summer in St. John's. It read, "Congratulations for passing with honours." For me it was a happy moment, both because I passed and because he cared enough to apprise me of the fact ahead of time.

Upon completing Junior Matriculation, I spent the following winter at Grand Falls with my father's sister, Aunt Bertha, who had married Uncle Ernest Thomas and produced a horde of small Thomases. Upon returning home via SS *Clyde* in the spring, it was to learn that Phil and Doris had married. Thus ended my first love's young dream, but with the resiliency of youth, I made a fairly rapid recovery.

By the time I was eighteen, Gladys had abandoned teaching for a nursing career. In her last year of Nurse's Training at the Grace Hospital, and largely due to her efforts, I was accepted into Nurse's Training also, in June 1936. Madge followed a couple of years later and eventually so did cousin Joyce. Our Donnie boy was about ten when I left home. He was an engaging little imp who along with Cyril, got into all sorts of mischief, but none of it malicious. My mother just doted on that boy, and when, years later, he lost the index finger of his right hand in an accident, she was shattered, but he made us all very proud when he rose above that handicap to become a successful dentist.

I was loath to leave my home, my family, and my beloved Island, and yet with the optimism and resiliency of youth, I impatiently awaited the day of departure. The day before I left, I wistfully visited some of my favourite haunts, saying goodbye to my childhood. As the ship steamed out of the harbour and headed for the open sea, I could see my mother, standing on our verandah, with apron to her eyes, waving wildly. I watched till she was no longer visible, then, drying my tears and filled with an incredible sense of well-being and expectancy, I bade silent farewell to the familiar landscape.

I was prepared to sail into the future, confident and unafraid, but I was so homesick that first year I was away, that only my sister Gladys's presence made it bearable. Gradually I became used to it, but the nostalgia has never left me. To this day I carry with me the memory of the sunlight dancing on the harbour waves, the tall schooners silhouetted in the moonlight, the rugged mountains in the background, the shady lanes where we picked wild violets, the giant dogberry trees growing out from the bare rock surface along the shore from our house, the grassy walks to Spencer's Dock, where the waves of Jerry's Run broke on the shores, and the silence of the everlasting hills.

Postscript

by Janice Wells

Gladys, Gwen, and Joyce led their nursing classes and Gladys and Gwen were valedictorians.

Gwen's nursing career included the Sanatorium and the American Army base Fort Pepperell in St. John's, until she was asked to help set up the new hospital at the US Air Force Base at Harmon Field, Stephenville. There she met all the American stars of the day, dancing with the likes of Frank Sinatra and Bob Hope. When the war was over, her spirit of adventure led her to DeGraff Memorial in North Tonawanda, New York, where she met and married Paul Molnar, a Hungarian-American restaurateur, began working with him in his business, and they had two children.

Gladys taught at the Grace Hospital before taking up a position in the Harbour Breton Cottage Hospital, where she met and married the medical officer in charge, Dr. Jim Paton, an Irishman who later became Sr. Medical Officer in Gander. The hospital there now is named after him in honour of his outstanding service to his patients and the health system in his adopted country. They had two children. Following Jim's early death from cancer, Gladys returned to full-time nursing in Gander.

Geneva taught in Clarke's Beach and Comfort Cove before her teaching career was ended by typhoid fever, which was nearly fatal. She went back to Pilley's Island to recuperate, and it was a slow and painful process. The Depression was on and Geneva eked out a living as a seamstress, putting her early talent to work as she made everything from tailored men's suits to a huge flag for a loggers union, appliquéd on both sides with an enormous bucksaw and a myriad of sharp teeth. During that time she started seeing Charlie Wells, the football hero of younger years and by then a woods contractor. They married, settling in Corner Brook, where they had three daughters, the middle one being me, Janice.

Madge began her nursing career at the Mental Hospital in St. John's, where her proficiency prompted an offer from the government to study further at Queen's University at the government's expense. A commitment of then giving two more years of service to Newfoundland was required and Madge turned it down to marry her handsome RCAF officer, Curtis Steeves, and move with him to Moncton, New Brunswick, where they raised five children and where she lives still.

Don graduated from Dalhousie University as a dentist, with busy practices first in Newfoundland and then in New Brunswick and Nova Scotia. His proficiency with his hands went beyond dentistry. He built two boats and became a skilled producer of intricately inlaid woodwork. He married Ann Gilliam and they had three sons.

Cyril was educated at Dalhousie University and the University of Toronto, receiving a doctorate in philosophy. He became a university professor and administrator, the editor-in-chief of volumes three to five of the *Encyclopedia of Newfoundland and Labrador*, an award-winning author, and a Member of the Order of Canada. He married Jean Parsons and they have three children.

Winston became an accountant in the financial industry, ending his working career as a senior bank official in Toronto. He married Marjorie Pike and they had two children.

Joyce began her career as Nurse in Charge at the cottage hospital in Bonne Bay, and later nursed in Niagara Falls and Toronto before joining Trans Canada Airlines as a flight attendant, for which at the time it was necessary to be a nurse. She married Wayne Danhof and settled in the States, where they had two children.

Following two years at Dalhousie University, Mervyn became an accountant, working on three continents. Following his marriage to Judy Young, he settled for a time in England, when ill health caused him to give up accounting, and he seriously pursued his love of landscape painting. He and Judy had three children.

Ed graduated from Dalhousie with a law degree and practiced law in Corner Brook until his retirement as senior partner in his firm. He married Marlene Penner and they had two sons.

Roy and Una, the two eldest Poole siblings from Dorm's first marriage, never left Pilley's Island. Roy never married and became caretaker of the school he had attended so reluctantly. Una married Ned Payne and raised a family of four just a few doors down from the house she grew up in.

The story of the Pooles and their life in Pilley's Island was enacted in many small outports along Newfoundland's coastline. While Newfoundland and Labrador's one-room schools produced thousands of accomplished men and women and an unusual number made their way into positions of prestige and power all around the world, when children excelled academically and went on to post-secondary education, most of the credit went to the parents. Intelligent, industrious, but basically illiterate men like Jesse and Dorm Poole supported their often better-educated wives (girls not being taken from school to work as often as boys) in their determination that their sons and daughters would be able to make their way in any world.

Although lacking formal education, my grandfather Jesse and great-uncle Dorm had an extraordinary sense of language. This, combined with my grandmother's and Blanche's love of literature, created a legacy as Cyril, Winston, Mervyn, Gwen, and Gladys became published writers of poems, essays, articles, or books. With a wonderful first novel soon to be published, Cyril's son Stephen joins me in the quest that my generation not let them down.

St. John's
2009

TO A NEWFOUNDLAND SEAMAN

Rude and unlettered as the world counts knowledge
Born to the sea, and tutored by the waves
His fortunes than the wind more variable,
Silently strong, his vessel's deck he treads.
Wedded is he, and bound to keep his vows
To this dark ship which leaps to do his will.
For him no sweated toil of dusty cities –
He dreams his long dreams on the pathless deep.

There are no words to capture that man's story
His face an epic is of gallant daring
And they who read may pause, and learn it there.
His soul is big, not having had to shrink
To fit the narrow boundaries of a warehouse.
He sees the world through eyes that, in their vision
Have held Orion and the lone North Star
Till lesser lights have faded from his view.
For life's immensity belongs to him
For all his sears the gift . . . son of the sea.

Gladys Poole
1938